THE POETRY OF STEVIE SMITH

LITTLE GIRL LOST

'The English are fanciful as they are also sensible.'
Stevie Smith

The Poetry of Stevie Smith

'Little Girl Lost'

ARTHUR C. RANKIN

1985
COLIN SMYTHE
Gerrards Cross, Bucks

BARNES AND NOBLE BOOKS
Totowa, New Jersey

First published in 1985 by Colin Smythe Limited
Gerrards Cross, Buckinghamshire

British Library Cataloguing in Publication Data

Rankin, Arthur C.
The poetry of Stevie Smith.
'Little Girl Lost'
1. Smith, Stevie—Criticism and interpretation
I. Title
821.912   PR6037.M43

ISBN 0-86140-187-5

First published in the United States of America
by Barnes and Noble Books, Totowa,
N.J.07512

Library of Congress Cataloging in Publication Data

Rankin, Arthur.
The poetry of Stevie Smith.
1. Smith, Stevie, 1902-1971—Criticism and
interpretation. I. Smith, Stevie, 1902-1971. II. Title.
PR6037.M43Z85   1985   828'.91209   84-16896
ISBN 0-389-20508-7

Produced in Great Britain
Designed by Leslie Hayward
Phototypeset by Grove Graphics, Tring, Hertfordshire
and printed and bound by Billing & Sons Limited,
Worcester

To Stella

Improvement makes strait roads, but the crooked roads without Improvement are roads of Genius.

William Blake

Contents

PREFACE

Only two critics have, so far, made a detailed study of Stevie Smith's work: Janet Watts in her introductions to the three novels when they were republished by the Virago Press in 1979–1980; and Hermione Lee in her long introduction to *Stevie Smith: A Selection* (Faber & Faber 1983). Both these critics have wonderfully illuminated the novels and the poetry and, I believe, have played their part in furthering appreciation of her work. There is though always room for another voice — provided it is a good one.

When Mr Rankin first showed me his book I was immediately impressed by his understanding of her work and of her as a person, clearly based on many years of exhaustive study. Above all I like his enthusiasm which he has the faculty of communicating. As Stevie Smith's executor, I am delighted he has found a publisher with the good sense to accept his book for it will extend readers' enjoyment of a remarkable poet who, only after her death, is being given her true niche in the assembly of major English poets.

James MacGibbon

FOREWORD

Stevie Smith was christened Florence Margaret; she was called Peggy
in her childhood and later adopted the sobriquet Stevie. Following
the precedent of Hugh Whitemore in his play *Stevie*[1], and of James
MacGibbon in his Preface to the *Collected Poems*[2], I have decided,
after some thought, to drop the surname throughout. I feel that this
is a special case, and that the constant reiteration of 'Stevie Smith',
or, worse still, of Miss Smith, would be immensely irritating to the
reader.

My thanks are due to Mr MacGibbon, Stevie Smith's Literary
Executor, for his kind permission to quote so freely from her written
work, and to reproduce a number of her drawings. I greatly
appreciate his encouragement in the venture.

Lastly I wish to express my profound gratitude to my wife Stella,
for her invaluable and patient help throughout, and also to my sister,
Janice M. Rankin.

A.R.

1. Hugh Whitemore. *Stevie: A play from the life and work of Stevie Smith*, French
   (London), 1977.
2. Stevie Smith, *The Collected Poems of Stevie Smith*, Allen Lane (London), 1975.

1

A Wild Civility

'The Hound of Ulster', which opens Stevie Smith's first volume of poems, sounds a plangent, eerie note that is wholly characteristic: no earlier poet had written anything quite like it. And like all of the poems placed at the beginning of each of her other seven volumes, it is a key-poem, revealing a particular slant on life.

The poem begins with a casual but deceptive innocence, and builds up to a shattering climax:

> Little boy
> Will you stop
> And take a look
> In the puppy shop —

and the speaker goes on to describe the various attractions of the dogs within. But the boy's reply has a quiver of suspicion:

> Thank you courteous stranger, said the child,
> By your words I am beguiled,
> But tell me I pray
> What lurks in the gray
> Cold shadows at the back of the shop?

With a sudden shock of awareness the stranger exclaims:

> Little boy do not stop
> Come away
> From the puppy shop.
> For the Hound of Ulster lies tethered there
> Cuchulain tethered by his golden hair

13

His eyes are closed and his lips are pale
Hurry little boy he is not for sale.[1]

Fate is not to be bargained with, and we never know what is round
the next corner.

Stevie Smith's poetry early attracted a small but devoted band of
readers, some of whom came to know it through her public readings.
Desmond MacCarthy, who died in 1952, declared that she had 'a
little nugget of genius'. This has not till recently been an established
view in literary circles for possibly two reasons: the first was her
habit of placing rather slight poems, some at first glance trivial,
alongside the finer ones; the second was the fact that the poems were
accompanied by drawings of a sort that has been described as 'the
higher doodling'. Despite the great precedent of Blake, there lingers
a strange prejudice against illustrating one's own work — even Philip
Larkin, in a warmly appreciative article in *The New Statesman*,
described the practice as 'the hallmark of frivolity'.[2] Consequently
the poems, themselves sometimes oddly disconcerting at a first
glance, were summarily dismissed as no more than *verbal* doodling.
But the drawings need no justification; they are often exquisite. One
has only to attempt to make tracings of them to discover that a single
line a hair's breadth out of place will ruin the whole composition.
They are often evocative, and sometimes add another dimension to
the poems they illustrate. Mr James MacGibbon has written, in his
Preface to the 'Collected Poems': 'I have her word for it that she
"doodled" these drawings, and, when it came to book publication,
she merely picked out such as seemed appropriate . . .'.[3] But I
myself suspect that those which are most cogent and evocative,
especially in the earlier volumes, represent the original inspiration
which came to her first in visual form, and later emerged in their
predestined literary form. I do not think it is possible to separate
poem from drawing in these instances, or to doubt that they are parts
of one conception. But in writing some of the later poems, she often
had to make do with drawings that were only more or less
appropriate.

From the late fifties, Stevie's poems began to appear in the weeklies
and Sunday papers, and her later volumes received discerning and
often enthusiastic critical appraisal. It was recognised that a new and

1. Stevie Smith, *The Collected Poems of Stevie Smith*, Allen Lane (London), 1975,
   henceforward called *Poems*, p. 15.
2. Philip Larkin, 'Frivolous and Vulnerable', review of *Selected Poems*, *New
   Statesman*, September 1962, pp. 416–8. Reprinted in his *Required Writing*, Faber
   & Faber, 1983.
3. *Poems*, p. 11.

original talent had arrived, and her reputation became established.
Nevertheless I have a suspicion that some of those who so slightingly
dismissed her in early years would be far from sorry to see her cut
down to size.

Perhaps Anthony Thwaite's account of her work, in his valuable
little book *Twentieth Century English Poetry* may be taken to
represent average open-minded critical opinion at the present time.
He describes her perceptively as 'a very special poet of strangeness,
loneliness and quirky humour . . . her blend of levity, loneliness
and sometimes asperity, was inimitable'.[1] This is admirable as far
as it goes, but I do not think it goes far enough. Professor Thwaite
does not, I feel, give sufficient recognition to the wide range of her
subject matter, to her profound human insight, to her religious quest,
to her lyrical magic, to her gift for compression, or to her astonishing
technical mastery.

Stevie's poetic diction, with all its idiosyncrasy is, in fact, her
greatest strength. Much contemporary verse, in getting rid of stale,
outworn poeticising, has sacrificed most of the essence of poetry.
However worth-while the thought, such verse is often hard to read:
one's attention tends to wander. But from the beginning Stevie
Smith's poetry showed a special gift for blending colloquial diction
with poetic feeling that was all her own. By the subtle use of
assonance and vowel music, by varying the length of the lines, by
way-out or internal rhyming, by delicate or daring syncopation, by
the odd, unexpected word, by sudden lapses into flat or banal
verbiage, by skilful punctuation or by the absence of punctuation,
she achieved an enchanting sense of flow and spontaneity. Her verse
sings and dances.

Stevie did not shrink from the judicious use of archaism, or from
employing the second person singular, which can easily become
oppressive, as occasionally in the nowadays unjustly neglected poetry
of Walter de la Mare, and which would certainly be out-of-place
in most contemporary verse. One wonders what growth of reserve
in the English character has led to its expulsion from our common
speech except in local pockets, when other countries have retained
the intimate form of address. In poetry its virtual disappearance is
surely an impoverishment. But Stevie, unlike de la Mare, never
indulged in 'poesy'.

Philip Larkin in his article on Stevie in the *New Statesman* wrote
that 'she sees something poetic move where we do not, takes a pot-
shot at it, and when she holds it up forces us to admit that there

1. Anthony Thwaite, *Twentieth Century English Poetry: An Introduction*,
Heinemann (London), 1978, pp. 86–7.

was something there, even though we have never seen anything like it before . . .'[1] This is beautifully put, and we know exactly what he means, and yet I doubt if Stevie ever took pot-shots; she knew perfectly well what she was about, and seldom missed the mark. In a similar vein, A. Alvarez, in a review of the *Collected Poems* in *The Observer* wrote amusingly that 'in poem after poem she starts solemn, but can't keep it up. Edward Lear had the same problem'.[2] But I doubt whether there was a problem in either case, and feel that Mr Alvarez was describing, in an oblique way, Stevie's brilliantly eccentric technique. He virtually conceded the point a few lines later: 'when she read her poems aloud they took on a marvellously shrewd elegance, shifting without effort from solemn to comic, from the grandest Victorian romance to owlish bathos'.[3] 'A marvellously shrewd elegance'. It could hardly be better put.

A word must be said concerning Stevie's debt to other poets. Apart from the pervasive influence of ballads and nursery rhymes, I do not think that there are many influences which can be indicated with any certainty. There is certainly an affinity with Coleridge, especially

1. *New Statesman*, 28 September 1962, p. 416.
2. A. Alvarez, 'Deadly Funny', review of *Collected Poems*, *Observer Review*, 3 August 1975, p. 21.
3. *Ibid.*

with the strange and uncanny element in his poetry. Occasionally there is a hint of Tennyson whom she greatly admired. And I think that Blake was often within hailing distance. His 'Proverb of Hell' which prefaces this book is of course, like most aphorisms, only one side of the coin, and, when applied to certain of his own writings, it might be considered to be special pleading. It need hardly be pointed out that 'strait' is no mispelling, but adroitly conveys a double meaning. As regards Stevie's metre, I feel that her frequent delicate shifting of stress, and sometimes her extended, wavering lines, may owe something to de la Mare, and also to Blake.

To borrow a term from astronomy, Stevie Smith might be described as an 'irregular variable', a term denoting a celestial luminary whose behaviour is erratic and unpredictable; but I do not think that she was a 'dwarf variable'.

2

This Heartless Mood

In this book I have sought to make a provisional appraisal of Stevie Smith's poetry, to elucidate its various aspects, and also to highlight poems of especial interest which may be in danger of being overshadowed. We know how all too often a few examples from a poet's output are quoted and anthologized again and again, whereas others of equal or possibly greater merit are left in the shade. The core of this chapter is an attempt to demonstrate something of her quality by setting one of her poems alongside some lines from an acknowledged masterpiece which expresses a precisely similar mood, though without claiming equality for Stevie's poem. But I will first cite a few very diverse short poems which do not fit comfortably under subsequent chapter headings but which are short enough to quote complete. The first of these might not be recognized immediately as hers, though on close examination I think that her hand is evident. The title is its first four words:

> When the sparrow flies to the delicate branch
> He seems to be a heavy one alighting there,
> It is March, and the fine twigs dance
> As the boisterous sparrow plunges masterfully.
>
> Fly again to my heart oh my beloved,
> My heart flies too high when you are absent.[1]

There is something of the economy of a Japanese print here, and the little poem lingers in the memory. The epigrammatic poem 'Reversionary' has her devastating 'scorpion' touch:

> The Lion dishonoured bids death come,
> The worm in like hap lingers on.
> The Lion dead, his pride no less,
> The world inherits wormliness.[2]

And here finally is one of her numerous poems based on classical themes, 'The Ambassador', which shows her ability to handle broadly-spanned blank verse:

1. *Poems*, p. 215.
2. *Ibid*, p. 124.

Underneath the broad hat is the face of
  the Ambassador
He rides on a white horse through hell
  looking two ways.
Doors open before him and shut when
  he has passed.
He is master of the mysteries and in the
  market place
He is known. He stole the trident, the
  girdle,
The sword, the sceptre and many
  mechanical instruments.
Thieves honour him. In the underworld
  he rides carelessly.
Sometimes he rises into the air and flies
  silently.[1]

This is a catalogue of the attributes of
Hermes, yet it is much more than the
sum of its parts. It sends shivers down
the spine — we are brought into the
presence of a god.

In comparing one of Stevie's poems with some lines of an
acknowledged masterpiece, Coleridge's *Dejection: A Letter*, I am not
attempting to put her beautiful, though not quite flawless poem on
a level with his majestic lines, from which I quote to refresh the
reader's memory:

> . . . In this Heartless Mood
> All this long Eve, so balmy and serene
> Have I been gazing on the western Sky
> With its peculiar Tint of Yellow Green —
> And still I gaze — and with how blank an eye! . . .

The passage ends with the heartbroken lines:

> I see them all, so excellently fair!
> I see, not feel, how beautiful they are.

Naturally Stevie was familiar with these lines, and she must have
been deeply moved by them. But I am convinced that, had she never

1. *Poems*, p. 247.

read them, she would still have written 'Every Lovely Limb's a
Desolation', which expresses, in quite another style and metre, a state
of consciousness exactly similar, and may be thought of as a feminine
counterpart of Coleridge's lines. It is necessary to quote at some
length:

> I feel a mortal isolation
> Wrap each lovely limb in desolation,
> Sight, hearing, all
> Suffer a fall.
>
> I see the pretty fields and streams, I hear
> Beasts calling and birds singing, oh not clear
> But as a prisoner
> Who in a train doth pass
> And through the glass
> Peer;
> Ah me, so far away is joy, so near . . .
>
> Yet there are days, oh brief,
> When thought's caught half-asleep
> (Most merrily) and drowsing
> Set in a meadow browsing.
>
> Ah then, like summer breeze in lovely trees
> That comes in little pants unequally,
> Or like the little waves of summer seas
> That push and fuss
> In heaven knows what sort of busyness,
> Idly, idly, my thoughts bring me to sleep,
> On sunny summer day to sleep. In sun
> I fall asleep . . .[1]

The poem narrowly misses perfection: it has a delicious freshness
and spontaneity, and an enchanting pattern. The dying fall of the
last lines quoted is magical. There is perhaps a touch of Wordsworth;
and certainly both this poem and Coleridge's are related in theme
to Wordsworth's great Ode which treats of the passing of the child's
capacity for visionary experience.

The poet is one who, to a greater degree than most, has succeeded
in preserving the innocent eye of childhood. Stevie wrote in a later
poem 'To Carry the Child'

> As the child has colours, and the man sees no

> Colours or anything,
> Being easy only in things of the mind,
> The child is easy in feeling . . .

But Stevie sometimes felt that the price to be paid for retaining the visionary gleam was intolerably heavy:

> The child in adult life is defenceless
> And if he is grown-up, knows it,
> And the grown-up looks at the childish part
> And despises it.[1]

How bitter then, while continuing to pay the price, to find that one is being robbed of the fruit: the joy and sustenance of sensory experience.

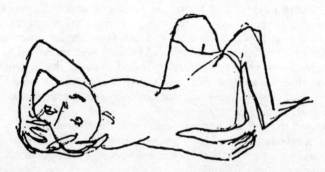

I have no doubt that Stevie felt a particularly close affinity with Coleridge. Both were denied the close human and sensuous relationship that they craved and both were, for long periods, cut off from the deep communion with nature which would, to some extent, have compensated for that loss. In both, the outgoing, life-giving forces were turned back on themselves, inwards and deathwards.

A passage from her second novel *Over the Frontier* conveys one of her black moods which she frequently had to endure:

> But the music grows faster, more slave-driving, more compelling. There is no rest, no pause . . . And always there is this pain at my heart . . . that is so rending and tearing, and always getting more and more. And within the music there is moving now a more insistent clamour, a harsh grating sound, a clashing of steel on

1. *Poems*, p. 436.

steel. It is very menacing, very military, this rapidly increasing metallic clamour, thrusting, drawing, marching.

Oh chords of immensity and insistence, waves of conflict from some deep hidden ocean bed . . . so hidden and so secret, sweeping up, licking and stretching, to cover and engulf some lonely seagirt promontory, come cover over then and make an end.

I am borne upright, suspended in the fathomless deep waters of a sombre and phosphorescent sea, swinging in silence and desolation between the poles of the world. How silent and sombre the deep swinging sea, swinging in malevolent intent upon its own storm basis of volcanic fury, what depths above me and below, how hellishly cold it is, how bitter and how solitary . . .[1]

This awe-inspiring passage like many passages in the three novels, is of course poetry, and poetry of no mean order. Its mood is coloured by her growing awareness of the darkness that was spreading over Europe, 'the scent of death' from the ever-increasing menace of Nazi Germany, which had become even more real to her through her visits to that country — 'these Germans, this lamentable people, that are so hysterical and docile and unfree — with their shining mad eyes — Freud said that Germany had the greatest death-wish in the world of any nation'.[2]

I suspect that, in her desperate moments, she always had the sense of being utterly cold and lost. 'Do you ever feel so cold, so frozen cold, and so far away, that love is a desperate chance clutch upon a hen-coop in mid-Atlantic?'.[3]

The aim of this book is not biographical: its purpose is to study the poetry itself, and I am especially averse to the idea of psychoanalytical probing. Yet, in examining the poetry and novels, I have found it unavoidable to point out the recurrence of certain themes, which sometimes amount to obsessions, and to try to throw some light on 'the core of hidden deep disturbance' revealed in so much of her work, by reference to what we know of Stevie's life.

1. Stevie Smith, *Over the Frontier*, Jonathan Cape (London), 1938, and Virago Press (London), 1980, pp. 49–50. Page references for both editions coincide.
2. Stevie Smith, *The Holiday*, Chapman & Hall (London), 1949 and Virago Press (London), 1979, pp. 87–8. Page references for both editions coincide.
3. *Ibid*, p. 49.

3
From the Earthquake Bed

Despite the excellent educational work done in many of our schools, and by the B.B.C. in its programmes of verse, poetry is still the Cinderella of the arts in this country. It is widely regarded as a peripheral activity, irrelevant to the serious business of living, mere trimmings, slightly ludicrous if not sissy, and is sometimes productive of derisive sniggers. The Welsh poet Danny Abse remarked not long ago in a television programme that in England a poet hesitates to declare himself as such.

Worse still, in the mental climate of our age, dominated by the strictly scientific approach to reality, there is prevalent a tabu on symbol and metaphor which the poet and critic, Kathleen Raine, in her elequent vindication of poetic tradition, *Defending Ancient Springs*[1], attributes to the parching influence of the Cambridge school of positivist philosophy. With such restrictions, inspiration is inhibited, and the deep archetypal patterns are unable to emerge. Moreover there is a tendency to frown on rhyme or even on marked rhythmic pattern, on incantation itself, which is surely the essence of poetry. The trend is analogous to the cult of social realism and minimalism which largely dominates the scene in the visual arts. In both fields there is, I suspect, a latent fear and dislike of beauty, often motivated by an unconscious sense of mediocrity in the critic himself.

Stevie Smith, for all her originality of thought and feeling, and for all her metrical daring, was in this respect an unabashed traditionalist and romantic. She was far too independent and, despite her diffidence, basically far too sure of herself, to pay heed to such devitalizing dogma. This, together with the fact that so many of her poems, simple, spontaneous and direct, bridge the gap between 'serious' and 'popular' verse, may be one reason why her work often appeals strongly to the younger generation.

In certain poems Stevie has revealed something of her own experience in the creative act: the invasion or possession by a power

1. Kathleen Raine, *Defending Ancient Springs*, Oxford University Press (London), 1967.

23

from the depths of her being. In 'Who is this Who Howls and Mutters?' she tells of the poet's attempt to stifle the insistent clamour from within:

> Who is this that howls and mutters?
> It is the Muse, each word she utters
> Is thrown against a shuttered door
> And very soon she'll speak no more . . .

The summons is ignored on the specious plea that the call is not loud enough — the Muse falls silent and departs. But becoming guilt-stricken the poet seeks the Muse 'by night and day', calling on the Lord to forgive the murder of talent, to repent and recall her Muse:

> He did repent. I have her now again
> Howling much worse, and oh the door is open.[1]

Such an eruption may not seem to accord with Wordsworth's famous dictum that poetry is 'emotion recollected in tranquility'. Professor D. G. James, in *Scepticism and Poetry*, has thrown much light on the act of creation. He writes of 'the process of objectification . . . whereby, as it were, the poet distances his emotional and conative reactions. It is not the case', he says, 'that they thereby differ in intensity: it is only that his self-consciousness seeks not to be diminished or swamped by strong emotion. However impassioned those experiences may be, the condition of great poetry is that they do not wholly possess him. *He* must seek actively to possess *them* . . . It is an active enjoyment, not a passive suffering, of his experiences . . . there must go on a certain depersonalization, a quietness in the midst of the speed of passion . . . Hence in lyrical poetry what is conveyed is not mere emotion, but the imaginative prehension of emotional states . . . which is a different thing'.[2] Thus, when the door is open, and the clamour of the Muse is stilled, a trance-like state takes over in which vision can fulfil itself.

There is another of Stevie's poems, a sad one, in which the poet persists in denying entry to the Muse, who reproaches him, but is not insistent enough to batter down his resistance. Sometimes creativity may be prostituted, or sacrificed for reasons of expediency. 'The Fairy Bell' tells of a renegade poet who, 'having taken to journalism for more money, is rebuked by his Muse in the form of an old gentleman; he cuts her throat':

1. *Poems*, p. 370.

2. David G. James, *Scepticism and Poetry: An Essay on the Poetic Imagination*, Allen and Unwin (London), 1937, pp. 112–13.

He seemed a melancholy but a reasonable creature,
Yet I could see about his hat as it were this belfry steeple.

The agony through which I go,
He said, is something that you ought to know
And something that you will know too
When I have finished telling you . . .

After brief rationalizing with himself, the poet proceeds to commit the fell deed:

It is done now and I cannot trouble to rue it,
I took his gullet in my hand and with my knife cut through it.

But still in my head I sometimes hear the soft tune
Of the belfry bats moaning to find more room
And the ding-dong of that imaginary sound
Is as grateful as a fairy bell tolling by waters drowned.[1]

It is distressing to have to truncate this beautifully proportioned and hauntingly musical poem.

When the creative impulse feels that it can sooner or later gain entry into consciousness, it howls and mutters until it can find expression. But sometimes it is enfeebled owing to adverse conditions, or owing to some flaw in the poet's make-up, and this may explain the Muse's strange personification here as an old gentleman. But if permanently stifled, the Muse allows the poet no rest, as we have seen in the first poem cited in this chapter.

The strangest and most compelling of this group is 'Look!' which treats in symbol of the act of creation as a process of discovery:

I am becalmed in a deep sea
And give signals, but they are not answered . . .

The poet is seeking direction, but the Muse is not ready to speak. The calm sea is surely the trance-like state — Wordsworth's 'tranquillity' — in which vision can be realized:

Into the dark night to darker I move
And the lights of the ships are not seen now
But instead there is a phosphorescence from the water.
That light shines, and now I see

1. *Poems*, p. 307.

Low down, as I bend my hand in the water
A fish so transparent in his inner organs
That I know he comes from the earthquake bed
Five miles below where I sail, I sail . . .
Into my hand he comes, the travelling creature,
Not from the sea-bed only but from the generations . . .[1]

This uncanny apparition is projected by an upheaval from the deep unconscious. He travels 'not from the sea-bed only but from the generations' for the reason that he is an archetypal figure.

We have Stevie's assurance that the impulse to write came only when she was unhappy. As one becomes more familiar with this rare and sensitive spirit, one feels thankful to know that at least she was able to seek solace and fulfilment in her art.

1. *Poems*, p. 369.

4

Footstep in the Sand

Forgive me forgive me for here where I stand
There is no friend beside me no lover at hand
No footstep but mine in my desert of sand.[1]

In Stevie's third novel *The Holiday*, which appears to be almost
entirely autobiographical, Celia is Stevie herself. Her uncle said that
in her early years she was 'the happiest child'. But after childhood
her life was haunted by a sense of alienation. She had a gift for
friendship, many and devoted friends, and was also a sociable person
who loved parties. 'I have never neglected the altars of Venus', she
wrote in *Novel on Yellow Paper*, 'nor avoided her *supplices*, certainly
I rate this goddess very highly and have never refused an
encounter.'[2] But after two early love affairs and one intense but
unfulfilled attachment, some sort of barrier prevented her from
finding the deep relationship which she longed for. In Hugh
Whitemore's beautiful play *Stevie*, she discovered that she and her
friend Karl were not suited to a lasting relationship, chiefly owing
to incompatibility due to the clash of nationality and culture. The
union with Freddy that followed was evidently deeper; it is viewed
from all angles in the poem 'Freddy'.[3] Both relationships were
rewarding but the second lasted longer: it was slower and more
painful in its dissolution. The poem 'I Like to Play with Him' may
refer to Freddy. It has a ring of immediacy:

Oh on that evening you were
So charming enchanting touching
Lost wounded and betrayed
Oh that should have been only the beginning.[4]

1. *Poems*, p. 23, 'Forgive me, forgive me'.
2. Stevie Smith, *Novel on Yellow Paper or: Work it out for Yourself*, Jonathan Cape
   (London), 1936, and Virago Press (London), 1980, p. 199. The page references
   of both editions coincide.
3. *Poems*, p. 65.
4. *Ibid.*, p. 53.

Incidentally, commas would have destroyed the spontaneity of the lines.

How much Stevie sacrificed by the eventual relinquishment of passionate love can be seen in a much later poem 'Votaries of Both Sexes Cry First to Venus':

> But one stood up and said: I love
> The love that comes in the dark fields,
> In the late night, in the hot breathless dark night:
> In the moony forest, when there is a moon,
> In the moony rides of the dark forest.
> I love this love: it is eerie if there is not
> *My* love in my *arms* then. It is exciting then,
> It is such an excitement as is on the approach
> Of Death . . .[1]

We will return to this poem in another chapter.

There are signs that the frustration of a later attachment left her with a sense of profound loss. The beautiful little poem 'The Boat',[2] though written earlier, reveals a capacity for intense devotion. Celia, in *The Holiday*, who is of course Stevie herself, is deeply attached to her cousin Caz (Casmilus), and their attachment is at the heart of the book. But unfortunately the actual degree of the blood-

1. *Poems*, p. 399.
2. *Ibid.*, p. 103.

relationship is in some doubt. That Caz is not a fictional character is confirmed in the introduction to her book *Cats in Colour*.[1]

Stevie's friend Kay Dick has quoted her as saying 'Being alive is like moving in enemy territory'.[2] She must have suffered torments from her extreme vulnerability. Her ultimate sense of isolation is expressed poignantly in 'Dirge':

> From a friend's friend I taste friendship,
> From a friend's friend love,
> My spirit in confusion,
> Long years I strove,
> But now I know that never
> Nearer shall I move,
> Than a friend's friend to friendship,
> To love than a friend's love.
>
> Into the dark night
> Resignedly I go,
> I am not so afraid of the dark night
> As the friends I do not know,
> I do not fear the night above,
> As I fear the friends below.[3]

1. *Cats in Colour*, introduced by Stevie Smith, Batsford (London), 1959, p. 14.
2. *Daily Telegraph Magazine*, 1 October 1971, p. 42.
3. *Poems*, p. 186.

'Love Me!' conveys, in imagination, an even greater descent into the depths. Its second stanza is disturbing, but it seems unlikely that the poem has, in any factual sense, a personal reference.[1]

Loneliness, or self-isolation is, of course, a central theme of the Romantic Revival. But Stevie's sense of isolation, her recurrent spells of melancholia, and her preoccupation with death, clearly had their source, at least in part, in traumatic experiences in childhood. She was volatile, subject to quicksilver changes of mood, and surprisingly resilient. The joy and excitement of living could push her dark obsessions into the background. So, in her writing, her mingling of pathos with zany humour is irresistible: fun and delight keep breaking through the melancholy — she was something of a Pierrot figure. One recalls Emily Dickinson's line 'Mirth is the mail of anguish'. While there is no doubt that, like so many artists, she had to suffer a crucifixion, yet she did have spells of intense happiness.

Stevie's father, partly owing to the influence of a domineering mother who constantly frustrated him, played a rather ineffectual rôle in his family, and eventually he disappeared altogether. But ultimately Stevie came to feel considerable sympathy with him. Her mother, though courageous, was probably insecure owing to her husband's unreliability and final desertion. On her early death the famous Lion Aunt took over the rearing of Stevie and her sister. She was a tower of strength, and there was a lifelong bond between her and Stevie. But the fact that she was a spinster, and rather conventional, must have had a negative effect on the two girls. Perhaps these lines from 'The Orphan Reformed' are relevant:

> The orphan is looking for parents
> She roams the world over
> Looking for parents and cover.
> She looks at this pair and that
> Cries, Father, Mother . . .

> At last the orphan is reformed. Now quite
> Alone she goes; now she is right . . .[2]

What is this but making the best of a bad job? The word 'cover' is revealing. Stevie was a snail without a shell.

The poem 'A Dream of Nourishment' seems to get to the heart of her sense of deprivation and lack of fulfilment more than any other, and I cannot think that it was by chance that she placed it

1. *Poems*, p. 191.
2. *Ibid.*, p. 241.

immediately after 'Every Lovely
Limb's a Desolation', which, as we
have seen, expresses so poignantly
the loss of the poet's capacity to
draw sustenance from the natural
world in all its richness and
beauty:

> I had a dream of nourishment
> Against a breast.
> My infant face was presst
> Ah me the *suffisance* I drew therefrom . . .
> For oh the sun of strength beat in my veins
> And swelled me full, I lay in brightest sun
> All ready to put forth, all bursting, all delight.
>
> But in my dream the breast withdrew
> In darkness I lay then
> And thin,
> Thin as a sheeted ghost . . .[1]

So concrete, so vivid is the
imagery that I feel that the
poem may describe an actual
happening either consciously
recalled or emerging from
below the threshold of
consciousness, for there are
those whose memory goes far
enough back to recall the
experience of birth itself, even
without the aid of hypnosis.
But it is also possible that the
image came to her as a
symbolic description of a state of being brought about by a number
of factors. Further, I am struck by the analogy between the
frustration of the power to draw nourishment from love-relationships
and from nature and the psychosomatic condition known as *anorexia
nervosa*, which inhibits the appetite for food. Sufferers from this

1. *Poems*, p. 344.

lamentable state believe that it has its source in guilt-feelings. It seems obvious that all sensory pleasures are related, and that a tabu on one might extend itself to others. The following chapter 'Angels' will, I think, demonstrate that Stevie as a child was deeply affected by religious doctrines of sin and punishment. But having taken all these factors into account, there is always the possibility that, in addition, she suffered from some functional, physical condition predisposing to depression.

5
Angels

> Poet, thou art dead and damned,
> That speakst upon no moral text.
> I bury one that babbled but; —
> Thou art the next, Thou art the next.[1]

At intervals throughout Stevie's earlier volumes of poems we encounter the awesome figures of Angels. These august beings are not invariably inimical. Sometimes as in 'Dream' and 'Angel of Grace'[2] they come to give warning. But they are usually severe, often cynical, or at best ironical. One cannot imagine that they would ever sing or dance as all good angels should. In 'Tableau de l'Inconstance des Mauvais Anges', the Angel in the drawing hovers significantly over a sharp-pointed rock and below a waning moon. Like 'The Hound of Ulster' he represents Fate and the unpleasant surprises that life is apt to spring on us. The text reads:

> Brightest and best are the sons of the morning,
> They wait on our footsteps and show us no ill.
> But waking or sleeping
> We are in their keeping
> And sooner or later they will do as they will.[3]

In 'Suicide's Epitaph' the Angel dispenses judgement pitilessly, rejecting the dead man's plea engraved on his tombstone:

1. *Poems*, p. 170.
2. *Ibid.*, pp. 37 and 64.
3. *Ibid.*, p. 152.

Oh Lord have mercy on my soul
As I had none upon my body.
And you who stand and read this rhyme
How do you do, Tomnoddy?[1]

'There, but for the grace of God, go you', the poor wretch seems
to be saying; 'I am only one of many'. But the angel is quite unmoved.
'Sois puni par où tu as tant péché, dit-il, en me regardant d'une
manière froide et enigmatique'.[2] Somehow the indictment sounds
all the more chilling delivered in French. The word 'enigmatique'
seems to suggest Stevie's perplexity concerning the nature of the
forces that control or invade life.

The frequent appearance of the Angels indicates a preoccupation
with sin, censure and punishment. It would point unmistakably to
the poet's having undergone a stern religious upbringing even if we
did not have her own words to prove it. In a letter to *Tribune* in
reply to Miss Dorothy Sayers, who challenged her concerning a book
review, Stevie wrote: 'I was taught, all go to hell who die in mortal
sin . . . Both my instructors and Miss Sayers agree that hell is (1)
everlasting, and (2) more painful than any pain known on earth or
to be imagined . . .'[1] She later challenged this appalling notion in
'Thoughts about the Christian Doctrine of. Eternal Hell':'

1. *Poems*, p. 155.
2. *Ibid.*
3. *Tribune*, 14 May 1948, p. 12.

The religion of Christianity
Is mixed of sweetness and cruelty
Reject this Sweetness, for she wears
A smoky dress out of hell fires . . .[1]

Stevie was a brilliant theological debater; but despite her acute probings and questionings of other aspects of Christian dogma it was surely, most of all, the refusal of the Anglican Church, to which she was powerfully drawn, to disown the doctrine of eternal punishment that prevented her from rejoining it. It was only after a long and arduous struggle that she succeeded, in some measure, in freeing herself from the tyranny that had been injected into her being. The little poem 'The Children of the Cross' depicts the agonizing ordeal:

Oh cold and ferocious are the children of the cross,
They have captured us and bound us and their gain is our loss.
But straining to death
In the stench of the fire's breath
We leave lonely for ever the children of the cross.[2]

In her fourth book of poems she turns to the attack, challenging and ridiculing the codified moralism of Christian orthodoxy, as in the poem 'No Categories!':

Plod on, you Angels say, do better aspire higher
And one day you may be like us, or those next below us . . .

Oh no no, you Angels I say
No heirarchies I pray.

Oh God, laugh not too much aside
Say not, it is a small matter.
See what your Angels do; scatter
Their pride; laugh them away . . .[3]

In this poem, with its dancing rhythm, is the liberating anti-moralism of Blake, of the Tao-Te-Ching, and of Jesus Christ himself: 'Judge not' and 'Consider the lilies of the field'. Here, with the conception of a God who is prone to merriment, is a turning-point in Stevie's quest for freedom. She has got the Accusers under at least partial

1. *Poems*, p. 387.
2. *Ibid.*, p. 150.
3. *Ibid.*, p. 258.

control. And a little poem in a later volume, 'The True Tyrant or the Spirit of Duty Rebuked', sets the seal on her liberation in replacing moralistic judgement with love:

> Then cried the lady from her kitchen
> Standing in her chains of grass:
> It is not Duty, it is Love
> That will not let me pass
> Evermore, evermore
> Through the grass-enchainèd door, the grassy door.[1]

'The Crown of Bays' is one of her strangest poems, touching on several of her major themes. It is a dialogue (one could almost describe it as a *pas-de-deux*) between a poet who, although he has just received acclaim, is disillusioned with life and with humanity, and the angel who is the donor of the award. The poet begs the angel for the gift of death, and after some argument, the latter consents and stabs him to the heart. The poem concludes:

> 'You receive what I do not know',
> Said the angel, and with this word
> Flies away and leaves him lying on the sward.
> But over his shoulder airborne came these last words; 'Briefly
> In my opinion for what it is worth, you die trivially'.[2]

In 'The Airy Christ: (After reading Dr Rieu's translation of St Mark's gospel)', Stevie depicts Jesus as a poet and singer. The poem has a lovely drawing:

> Those who truly hear the voice, the words, the happy song,
> Never shall need working laws to keep from doing wrong.
>
> Deaf men will pretend sometimes they hear the song, the words,
> And make excuse to sin extremely; this will be absurd.
>
> Heed it not. Whatever foolish men may do the song is cried
> For those who hear, and the sweet singer does not care that he was crucified.
>
> For he does not wish that men should love him more than anything
> Because he died; he only wishes they would hear him sing.[3]

1. *Poems*, p. 419.
2. *Ibid.*, p. 277.
3. *Ibid.*, p. 345.

'Was He Married?' is a pungent satire on the orthodox conception of Christ, and 'Oh Christianity, Christianity',[1] a formidable challenge to the doctrine of the incarnation and crucifixion. Strongly attracted though she was to the Anglican Church, such doctrinal objections weighed heavily in the scale in preventing her from becoming reconciled to it. And not only intellectually was she held at a distance; she also felt instinctively that there was something in Christian theology that did not ring true. There is a passage in *The Holiday* which is relevant:

> . . . It too much bears the mark of our humanity, this Christian religious idea, it is too tidy, too tidy by far. In its extreme tidy logic it is a dimunution and a lie. These rewards and punishments,

1. *Poems*, pp. 389, 416–17.

this grading, this father-son-teacher-pupil idea, it too much bears the human wish for something finished off and tidy . . . It is the most tearing and moving thing, this wish to gain marks and approval, to plod on, with personal and loving chastisement, to infinity. This beating idea is also something that is always coming up. The truth is that people cannot bear not to be beaten.

I read Father D'Arcy's book in proof, said Tom. When I had finished it I said: I don't believe a word of it . . .

It cannot be like this I said, it is not possible.[1]

And yet with all this, her affection for certain aspects of the Church, and perhaps most of all her craving to belong, remained. She described herself as 'an Anglican agnostic'. She loved the majestic poetry of the Authorized Version of the Bible, and the traditional version of the Book of Common Prayer, and in a poem recently quoted in a leading article in *The Daily Telegraph* she demanded:

Why are the clergy of the Church of England
Always altering the words of the prayers in the Prayer Book?
Cranmer's touch was surer than theirs, do they not respect him?
. . .[2]

1. *The Holiday*, 1949 and 1979, p. 43.
2. *Poems*, p. 335, 'Why are the Clergy . . .?'.

Had she lived into our times, one can imagine the withering scorn with which she would have denounced and derided the General Synod's Series 111, with its flat, uninspiring verbiage, and its total failure to communicate the poetic vision which is at the heart of religion.

She herself can occasionally speak with the voice of a minor prophet, as her in *Novel on Yellow Paper*: 'I feel I am an instrument of God, that is not altogether the Christian God; that I am an instrument of this God that must *calcine these clods*, that are at the same time stupid and vulgar, and set free this God's prisoners, that are swift, white and beautiful and very bright and flaming-fierce.'[1] Like Blake, in *The Everlasting Gospel*, she spurned false humility 'creeping Jesus', but her work shows throughout the self-knowledge which goes hand-in-hand with true humility.

1. *Novel on Yellow Paper*, 1936 and 1980, pp. 184–5.

6

The Lost Ones

To be lost in one way or another, and whether by choice or not, is a theme that occurs over and over again in the poems. In her first volume, in 'Up and Down'[1] and in the delightful 'Suburb', Stevie expresses a longing to separate herself from human contacts, or at least from the presence of the crowd:

How nice it is to slink the streets at night
And taste the slight
Flavour of acrity that comes
From pavements throwing off the dross
Of human tread.
Each paving-stone sardonic
Grins to its fellow-citizens masonic:
'Thank God they're gone', each to the other cries
'Now there is nothing between us and the skies'[2]

And in one of her late poems 'Scorpion' she flatly declares that she would prefer to be apart even when buried:

1. *Poems*, p. 31.
2. *Ibid.*, p. 81.

Sea and *grass* must be quite empty
Other souls can find somewhere *else* . . .[1]

In 'Lightly Bound' a young wife cries:

You beastly child, I wish you had miscarried,
You beastly husband, I wish I had never married.
You hear the north wind riding fast past the
   window? He calls me.
Do you suppose I shall stay when I can go so
   easily?[2]

'The Small Lady', wedded so it would seem,
to domesticity and progress — typified by her
highly-prized, labour-saving washing machine —
is tempted by 'a great witch passing on the air'.

. . . 'What is it you still wish for, my pretty dear?
Would you like to be a duck on a northern lake,
A milky white duck with a yellow beak? . . .'

The lady stoutly bids the witch begone:

   'Human inventions help properly, magic is a
      disgrace'.

But alas!

   The Witch flew off cackling for the harm was done.
   'I smell water', cried the lady and followed her into the setting
      sun.
   And now in a false shape, on the wind-driven black pelt
   Of that far northern lake, she is without help . . .[3]

This is a tale of total loss. There are cross-currents involved: on the
one hand home and comfort versus the lure of remote places, such
as tempts people to buy derelict cottages in distant parts, or to settle
on inhospitable islands, on the other the risk in getting involved with
the magical and occult. In introducing the ballad 'The Frozen Lake'

1. *Poems*, p. 513.
2. *Ibid.*, p. 266.
3. *Ibid.*, p. 471.

in a recording,'[1] Stevie spoke of 'the danger of traffic with the fairy wood'. And in the same recording, concerning one of the most beautiful of her 'legendary' poems, with a mediaeval atmosphere, 'I rode with my darling' she said of the narrator 'She chose to be lost':

> The wind bent the corn and drew it along the ground
> And the corn said, Do not go alone in the dark wood.
>
> Then the wind drew more strongly and black clouds covered
>   the moon
> And I rode into the dark wood at night . . .[2]

Throughout all these poems darkness, wind, ice, the far north, sunset, the thick and gloomy forest, the watery depths, the nether regions, are recurrent symbols. But not always is the loss absolute; There are poems in which isolation and sacrifice are turned to ultimate gain and self-discovery. One such is 'Persephone', one of a number of poems which embody mythical or classical themes. As we know, this daughter of Demeter, Queen of the tranquil and abundant Earth, was snatched away by Dis, Prince of the Underworld and carried down into his subterranean realm. Stevie gives the story a new slant. Persephone, though devoted to her mother, has all the time been restless and unfulfilled, and was herself a willing party to the kidnapping:

> Oh can you wonder can you wonder
> I struck the doll-faced day asunder
> Stretched out and plucked the flower of
>   winter thunder? . . .

In losing her sunlit and easeful life she finds her true 'shape':

> I in my new land learning
> Snow-drifts on the fingers burning,
> Ice, hurricane, cry: No returning.
>
> Does my husband the King know, does he
>   guess,
> In this wintriness
> Lies my happiness?[3]

1. *Listen* (The Marvell Press) unfortunately deleted.
2. *Poems*, p. 260.
3. *Ibid.*, pp. 248–9.

We have encountered here one more of the great themes of the Romantic Revival. In Blake it is expressed as Reason versus Energy, his 'Heaven' and 'Hell'. In at least two studies of Coleridge[1] 'Kubla Khan' is interpreted on similar lines, the irruption of the torrent of poetic vision into the formal garden of the Augustan Age. And Lord David Cecil in his *Early Victorian Novelists*[2] found a similar polar opposition in *Wuthering Heights*. Stevie's poem, despite a touch of flippancy in the first stanza, has brilliant impetus and masterly compression. But of all these poems, perhaps the one that goes deepest into the heart of her creative being is 'Voices about the Princess Anemone'. The drawing shews a young girl lying in the grass under the forest trees and gazing into the water of a stream, and I think that here we encounter Stevie herself, no less. In his preface to *The Collected Poems* Mr James MacGibbon describes Stevie's 'little-girl-look', 'her dark straight page-boy hair and dark eyes set in a pale mobile face . . . an almost sprite-like appearance'.[3] These are reflected in the drawing where she is disrobed, possibly to symbolize total self-revelation of spirit. The rather close parallel to the opening scene of Maeterlinck's and of Debussy's *Pelléas and Mélisande* is interesting. It will be recalled that Golaud, lost in the thick forest while hunting, hears a girl crying; he finds her at the water's edge. She is terrified and distraught, and, in reply to his questioning, tells him that *everyone* has hurt her. (She has been 'moving in enemy territory'). Her crown is shining in the water, where it has fallen. It is possible that Stevie had this scene in the play in mind, or was prompted by an unconscious recollection of it. But Anemone has possession of her crown, — her band of gold — perhaps she has retrieved it from the water. This key poem must, I think, be given complete:

Underneath the tangled tree
Lies the pale Anemone.

She was the first who ever wrote
The word of fear, and tied it round her throat.

She ran into the forest wild
And there she lay and never smiled.

1. See George G. Watson, *Coleridge the Poet*, Routledge, Kegan, Paul (London), 1966; and Geoffrey Yarlott, *Coleridge and the Abyssinian Maid*, Methuen (London), 1967.
2. See David Cecil, *Early Victorian Novelists: Essays in Revaluation*, Constable (London), 1934 and Collins (London), 1970.
3. Preface to *Collected Poems*, p. 9.

Sighing, Oh my word of fear
You shall be my only dear.

They said she was a princess lost
To an inheritance beyond all cost.

She feared too much they said, but she says, No,
My wealth is a golden reflection in the stream below.

She bends her head, her hands dip in the water
Fear is a band of gold on the King's daughter.[1]

This strange little poem is beautifully shaped: note how the
lengthening of certain lines reinforces their significance, especially
in the last two couplets. Stevie is surely saying that her haunting
anxiety and her sense of isolation are central to her poetic inspiration.
Her 'word of fear' is heard in many of her finest dramatic poems:
in 'I rode with my darling', in 'Songe d'Athalie' and in
'Eulenspiegelei':[2] the two last will be discussed in a later chapter.

1. *Poems*, p. 295.
2. *Ibid*., pp. 260, 324 and 98. The two last will be discussed in a later chapter.

The touching poem 'Oh Pug' is one of her last poems. It is as apposite to her as it is to the pet dog in question:

> You are an old dog now
> And in all your life
> You have never had cause for a moment's anxiety,
> Yet,
> In those great eyes of yours,
> Those liquid and protuberant orbs,
> Lies the shadow of immense insecurity. There
> Panic walks.
>
> Yes, yes, I know,
> When your mistress is with you,
> When your master
> Takes you upon his lap,
> Just then, for a moment,
> Almost you are not frightened.
>
> But at heart you are frightened, you always have been . . .[1]

1. *Poems.*, p. 547.

7

The Sting in the Tail

None of Stevie's three novels aspires to a plot, but they contain a gallery of sharply etched characters; *The Holiday* in particular is full of pathos, irony, paradox, strange or comical anecdotes and, in addition, much lively and forthright discussion of a variety of themes, the English character, the middle classes, the post-war scene, India, the ending of colonialism among them. In addition it is saturated with poetic feeling. Stevie could, I think, have excelled as a writer of short stories had she wished. Indeed, a few of the longer poems, 'The House of Over-Dew' and 'Angel Boley'[1] are versified narratives, and many of the shorter poems are short stories in embryo. Her keen observation of human nature in all its diversity — its comicality, sadness, violence and perversity — found expression in a host of thumbnail sketches, pathetic, acerbic and sometimes devastating. 'Scorpion', the title of her last volume and of the poem that opens it[2] was, like 'The Princess Anemone', one of her names for herself, and many of her poems in this category are veritable scorpions. In 1971 there appeared in *The Times Literary Supplement* a review, appreciative and discerning, but under the strangely inept heading 'The Voice of Genteel Decay'. The image of Stevie as a petit-bourgeois suburban spinster may possibly linger even now in some quarters; but to read just one bizarre and far from

1. *Poems*, pp. 553 and 530.
2. *Ibid.*, p. 513.

genteel poem, 'A Jew who is Angry with his Friend who does not believe in Circumcision' should be enough to dispel it:

'You look a little pale? What ho, a knife, a knife.'[1] The poem is illustrated by a comically fearsome little drawing.

There are poems about young ladies whom one would prefer not to encounter, such as 'Girls'!

> Girls! I will let down the side if I get a chance[2]
> And I will sell the pass for a couple of pence.

Equally unappealing is the girl in 'The Wedding Photograph'

So smile Harry smile and I will smile too
Thinking of what is going to happen to you,
It is the death wish lights my beautiful eyes
But people think you are lucky to go off with such a pretty prize
. . .[3]

1. *Poems*, p. 280.
2. *Ibid.*, p. 167.
3. *Ibid.*, p. 425.

No less deadly are some of the men portrayed such as 'The Murderer', 'Lord Barrenstock', and 'Major Macroo'[1]. 'Infelice' is a little masterpiece: it concerns a girl who is being ruthlessly exploited:

> One night he came, it was four in the morning,
> Walking slowly upstairs, he stands by my bed.
> Dear darling, lie beside me, it is too cold to stand speaking,
> He lies down beside me, his face is like the sand,
> He is in a sleep of love, my heart is singing.
> Sleeping softly softly, in the morning I must wake him,
> And waking he murmurs, I only came to sleep.
> The words are so sweetly cruel, how deeply he loves me . . .[2]

There are two poems concerning male inadequacy: one, 'The Afterthought' is an entertaining variant of the Rapunzel story. Here, the lover is somewhat lacking in ardour, and scarcely deserves our sympathy:

> Rapunzel Rapunzel let down your hair
> It is I your beautiful lover who am here
> And when I come up this time I will bring a rope ladder with me
> And then we can both escape into the dark wood immediately.

But off he goes into a winding course of speculation:

> This must be one of those things, as Edgar Allan Poe says
>   somewhere in a book,
> Just because it is perfectly obvious one is certain to overlook.
> I wonder sometimes by the way if Poe isn't a bit introspective,
> One can stand about getting rather reflective . . .

One can indeed, and wondering is all the fellow is capable of; but eventually he is made aware of the fact that the poor girl is becoming anxious:

> What is that darling? You cannot hear me?
> That's odd. I can hear you quite distinctly.[3]

This delightful poem is one of Stevie's wittiest. Another, 'Oh if Only' concerns 'an intellectual Englishman' who finds his girlfriend Blah in bed with a certain Captain Thomas:

1. *Poems*, pp. 117, 69 and 72.
2. *Ibid.*, p. 107.
3. *Ibid.*, p. 256.

Go to hell, cried Thomas. Go to hell, cried the young intellectual.
A purely nervous situation for you I fancy, sneered Thomas.
The young intellectual crept weeping away,
Oh, if he could only experience emotional extravagence![1]

This lover elicits our sympathy, even though it is plain that he is
well quit of Miss Blah. His deficiency is unfortunately not rare.

'The English' is equally penetrating; it illuminates what is perhaps
the negative aspect of the English genius for compromise:

Many of the English,
The intelligent English,
Of the Arts, the Professions and the Upper Middle Classes,
Are under-cover men,
But what is under the cover
(That was original)
Died; now they are corpse-carriers.
It is not noticeable, but be careful,
They are infective.[2]

This shrewd commentary may, I think, throw light with advantage
on our present political and sociological scene.

Several poems tell of relationships that are flawed, declining or
already dead. Such are the sad, ludicrous 'The Jungle Husband', the
acrid 'Le Désert de l'Amour',[3] and 'The-Devil-My-Wife':

Gush, then, gush and gabble,
Vanity is your dabble,
And in mediocrity
Is your cruelty.[4]

In the 'Listen' recording, now unfortunately unobtainable except in
some libraries, Stevie commented: 'You may think that the husband
here is rather cruel, but he is telling the truth. It is mediocrity that
makes things so suffering for others'. She returns frequently to this
theme, not referring so much to a lack of talent as to a meanness
of spirit. The Underground is for her a symbol of non-entity, as in
Over the Frontier: Man should be more than a 'strap-hanging season
ticket-holder' . . . he must 'go right forward and be a shining bright

1. *Poems*, p. 290.
2. *Ibid.*, p. 359.
3. *Ibid.*, pp. 332 and 120.
4. *Ibid.*, p. 198.

sword and maybe a disaster, if it comes to it he may be this disaster, but he will not be a little bloody squit that only asks please not to be noticed but to let pass in the crowd'.[1]

But her most biting portrait of mediocrity is 'The Face':

There is a face I know too well,
A face I dread to see,
So vain it is, so eloquent
Of all futility.

It is a human face that hides
A monkey soul within,
That bangs about, that beats a gong,
That makes a horrid din.

Sometimes the monkey soul will spread
Athwart the human eyes,
And peering forth, will flesh its pads,
And utter social lies.

So wretched is this face, so vain,
So empty, and forlorn,
You may well say that better far
This face had not been born.[2]

The drawing shows a vacuous, straw-hatted *flâneur* ambling along the street, with his cane.

In *Novel on Yellow Paper* Freddy says 'Bring your ideas down to earth. You want sense knocked into you. Keep your feet on the ground . . . You should.' Pompey (that is to say, Stevie herself) goes on:

'But now chaps is not this the very language of Mr Mere that is so very mere like I was telling you that is Mr Mere that would say to the Lord that would have said: My dear Jesus Christ, my advice to you is to bring your ideas down to earth don't, above all don't be hysterical. Keep your feet firmly on the ground. Plain ordinary men like you and me don't want to go gallivanting after these far-fetched ideas. It's indigestion thats what it is.'

All this starts her off into a brief prose poem that is too fine to be omitted:

'Oh Jesus Christ, in the mighty sweep of your divine mind, the

1. *Over the Frontier*, 1938 and 1980, p. 51.
2. *Poems*, p. 175.

sorrow of night space and the rushing air, the dark night and the soft plumage of the bird flying by night that brushes your exalted cheek, the wide and lofty thought sweeping ever upwards and outwards, bearing with it what agony of spirit and noble strife . . .'[1]

Devouring maternal love is revealed in 'N'est-ce pas assez de ne me point haïr?'[2] and in 'I'll have your heart':

> I'll have your heart, if not by gift my knife.
> Shall carve it out. I'll have your heart, your life.[3]

The daughter in the beautiful little drawing is adolescent. Stevie later omitted the second, longer stanza — a cry of numbed desolation from one whose capacity for love has been destroyed. In the deleted recording Stevie read 'Pad, pad' in which a former, rejected lover's bitterness is muted by age:

> Ah me, the power to feel exaggerated, angry and sad
> The years have taken from me. Softly I go now, pad, pad.[4]

And in the currently available Argo recording, she has read most touchingly 'The Repentance of Lady T':

1. *Novel on Yellow Paper*, 1936 and 1981, p. 221.
2. *Ibid.*, p. 217.
3. *Ibid.*, p. 148.
4. *Ibid.*, p. 253.

I look in the glass
Whose face do I see?
It is the face
Of Lady T.

I wish to change,
How can that be?
Oh Lamb of God
Change me, change me.[1]

Of two more short tragic Poems,
'The Sea-widow'[2] is I think well
known 'Her-zie' perhaps less so. It is
a ballad in brief, in which 'A troll and
his wife speak of the human child
they stole', the troll language being
suggested by the addition of an extra
syllable 'zie':

A hearse for Her-zie
Came for her.

What colour was it then?
Golden, golden,
Was there anyone in it?
A pale king was in it.
That was not a hearse for Her-zie, husband,
It was her marriage carriage.
It was a hearse for me, then,
My heart went with them and died then . . .[3]

These poems, the first read by Stevie herself, and both by Glenda
Jackson, in the Argo recordings, are profoundly impressive.

'Silence and Tears' is a revelation of hypocrisy. In the
aforementioned deleted recording, Stevie described it, with a barely
audible chuckle, as 'a terrible poem'. It is prefaced by an extract 'From
a church outfitter's catalogue: A priestly garment, suitable for
conducting funeral services in inclement weather'. Who but Stevie
would have thought of browsing in such unpromising literature? The
poem is a bitingly satirical but at the same time comical little
masterpiece:

1. *Poems*, p. 199.
2. *Ibid.*, p. 569.
3. *Ibid.*, p. 541.

And may the coffin hold his bones in peace that lies below,
And may the widow woman's tears make a good show,
And may the suitable priestly garment not let the breath of
   scandal through.

For the weather of their happening has been a little inclement,
And would people be so sympathetic if they knew how the
   story went?
Best not put it to the test. Silence and tears are convenient.[1]

The drawing too is masterly. The unctuous piety of the priest, the
assumed grief of the widow, the dreadfully bored little girl, the
expressions of the three top-hatted mourners, two exchanging barely
hidden cynical glances, and the excruciating discomfort of the third
— all these are contained in a design of perfect symmetry.

1. *Poems*, p. 110.

8

The Burnt Grass

In the early sixties there occurred a remarkable event which should not be allowed to be forgotten. Owing to a volcanic eruption on Tristan da Cunha, the inhabitants were forced to evacuate their island, and were transported to England. After experiencing the social and technological blessings of an advanced civilisation over a period of time, they reacted so strongly against these that all but a very few chose to return to their remote, windswept island. *The Daily Telegraph*, in a leading article entitled 'Is Britain Habitable?'[1], suggested that this astonishing preference should induce us to take another look at our vaunted technological and over-populated society.

In 'Alone in the Woods' Stevie felt that nature herself resented the impact of human invasion, and went on to say that man's 'gaudy mind' drives his body 'More and more in the wrong direction'[2]. Some have begun to wonder, in recent years, if the human species has not now reached pest proportions. Did Jehovah, perhaps, in the ancient myth, slip up disastrously in preserving Noah and his family? In the poem 'In Protocreation' Stevie painted pre-history in a few graphic brush-strokes, and went on to try out the notion that man is supererogatory:

> Oh had it but stopped then
> Oh had there not come men.
> In that high and early time
> There was no good deed and no crime
> No oppression by informèd mind
> No knowledge and no human kind.[3]

Man's informèd mind', which gives primacy to the rational and analytical faculties at the expense of feeling and imagination, has surely created a perilous imbalance in human consciousness. In *The*

1. 11 September 1962.
2. *Poems*, p. 32.
3. *Ibid.*, p. 284.

Holiday Stevie wrote, with characteristic and delightful paradox: 'I think that the intellectuality . . . runs mostly with the twenty-to-fifty years of man, and that the *instinctuality* that brings with it so much glee, so much pleasure that cannot be told, so much of a vaunting mischievous humility, so much of a truly imperial meekness, runs with childhood and old age'.[1] The beautiful poem 'Fafnir and the Knights', one of her own favourites, is surely symbolic of man's ruthless onslaught on Nature, both in himself and in his environment:

> Fafnir, I shall say then,
> Thou art better dead
> For the Knights have burnt thy grass
> And thou could'st not have fed.[2]

But Stevie, like Whitman, always reserved the right to contradict herself. In 'God and Man' she declared that man, far from being a blunder of the creative force, is God's 'darling', his 'all', the growing-point of creation[3], and in 'Touch and Go' she is desperately concerned that he win through[4]. In 'Away, Melancholy' she makes an eloquent case for man, who

> Beaten, corrupted, dying
> In his own blood lying
> Yet heaves up an eye above
> Cries, Love, love.
> It is his virtue needs explaining,
> Not his failing.[5]

Man's deepest longing is directed towards the good. That is what philosophers of old, such as Mencius, meant when they affirmed that the good in man is more fundamental than the evil: 'Man's nature is good, as water flows down'. The word 'wicked', according to Skeat, was originally a past participle, meaning 'rendered evil', from the obsolete adjective 'wikke' — we now have the colloquial expression 'bent'. This must surely indicate that we feel instinctively that wickedness is either a distortion of normal human nature, or else a stooping from what man was intended to be, from his potential stature.

1. *The Holiday*, 1949 and 1979, p. 124.
2. *Poems*, p. 323.
3. *Ibid.*, p. 261.
4. *Ibid.*, p. 235.
5. *Ibid.*, p. 329.

Something must be said concerning Stevie's devotion to animals: it is doubtful if any other poet has been so preoccupied with the mystery of animal life. In the Introduction to her book *Cats in Colour* she stressed the differences between animals and human beings at the expense of what they have in common: 'To look in an animal's eyes is to be aware of stupidity, so blank and shining these eyes are, so cold. It is mind that lights the human eyes, but what mind have animals? We do not know, and as we do not like not to know, we make up stories about them, give our thought and feelings to our poor pets, and then turn in disgust if they catch, as they sometimes do, something of our own fevers and unquietness. Tamed animals can grow neurotic, She went on to quote from her poem 'A Shooting Incident':

Wild creatures' eyes, the colonel said,
Are innocent and fathomless, . . .
But in the tame variety
There couches an anxiety
As if they yearned, yet knew not what
They yearned for, nor they yearned for not.
And so my dog would look at me
And it was pitiful to see
Such love and such dependency.

The human heart is not at ease
With animals that look like these[1]

Yet in another poem, she declares of the city dog 'his intelligence
is on the brink of human intelligence'; and there is a beautiful passage
in *The Holiday*:

'And there stood the great ape . . . there he stood in his shaggy
coat, standing on his hind legs to look with such a loving look
at his kind mistress, and the lady's face was close to the ape's face,
and there was this animal barrier between them, and yet affection
and trust.

And this lady said how the apes were bossy and moody and
jealous and wild, and yet uncomplicated by trying to be something
else. Yet in the dark eyes of the animal was real fondness. And
I thought: It is not so difficult for them, but we have come further
than the apes and know what we are and do not like it and want
to be something else. And I thought: We have come some way
from the apes, but we think we have not come far enough, and
so fall into abuse and despair.'[2]

A mischievous little poem 'The Listener', inspired by a talk on the
radio, 'An Encounter with Mosquitoes in New Guinea, by Miss
Cheeseman', certainly goes rather far in declaring:

. . . Their battles are as ours, as ours,
They are no different from our own . . .[3]

The redoubtable lady, when bitten all over, probably did not see
the matter from that angle.

But how does Stevie reconcile the love in the eyes of the colonel's
dog, and in those of the great ape, with the assertion that the eyes
of all animals are blank and cold? One wonders if she knew of the
work of the great naturalist Konrad Lorenz in his study of greylag
geese. Lorenz has told how a goose that has lost its mate is ravaged
with all the signs of passionate grief. As for intelligence, it would
seem that she had not heard of the chimpanzees who are said to be
capable of producing paintings of genuine merit, displaying a grasp
of design. And though she felt that people are too ready to attribute

1. *Cats in Colour*, pp. 7–8, and *Poems*, pp. 242–5.
2. *The Holiday*, 1949 and 1979, p. 64.
3. *Poems*, p. 451.

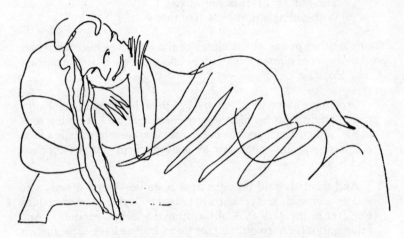

human feelings to their pets she yet proceeded to do just that in some of the comments appended to the photographs of cats in her book.

Certainly she was right in saying that we sometimes make our pets neurotic: '. . . all tamed animals are nervous, we have given them reason to be, not only by our cruelty but by our love too, that presses upon them'[1]. And in 'Nature and Free Animals' God pronounces

> I will forgive you everything,
> But what you have done to my Dogs
> I will not forgive.
> You have taught them the sicknesses of your mind
> And the sicknesses of your body
> You have taught them to be servile
> To hang servilely upon your countenance
> To be dependent touching and entertaining . . .[2]

But the dog Belvoir, the subject of two poems, would not have been so noble a creature without man's conditioning:

> Belvoir thy coat was not more golden than thy
> heart . . . [3]

In the last resort Stevie might, I think, have conceded that man's

1. *Cats in Colour*, p. 12.
2. *Poems*, p. 42.
3. *Ibid.*, p. 63.

moulding of domestic animals was, on the whole, an act of co-operation with nature rather than the reverse.

Although she was capable of teasing her pets, she abhorred the infliction of suffering on animals, as is shown in her denunciation of keeping wild animals in cages in 'The Zoo' and of circuses in 'This is Disgracefaul and Abominable'[1]. One can imagine her biting condemnation of certain experiments on animals which have come to light recently, motivated in some cases, by cold-blooded scientific curiosity[2], in others (and on a vast scale) by purely commercial interests. Another scathing attack on the callous treatment of animals is 'The Best Beast of the Fat-Stock Show at Earls Court':

> Slam the lift door,
> Push it up with a groan,
> Will they kill the Beast now?
> Where has he gone?
>
> When he lay in the straw
> His heart beat so fast
> His sides heaved, I touched his side
> As I walked past.
>
> I touched his side,
> I touched the root of his horns;
> The breath of the Beast
> Came in low moans.[3]

1. *Poems*, pp. 172–3 and 338.
2. See Theodore Roszak, *Where the Wasteland Ends: Politics and Transcendence in Post — Industrial Society*, Faber (London), 1973.
3. *Poems*, p. 413.

Poems about cats abound in her verse. 'The Singing Cat'[1] is fairly well-known, and has probably found its way into school anthologies; it deftly avoids sentimentality. 'The Galloping Cat' 'which gallops about doing good' is one of her zaniest poems. For once, one's sympathies are on the side of the Angel in this encounter[2]. To conclude, here is part of the 'Friends of the River Trent (At their Annual Dinner)':

> A dwindling body of ageing fish
> Is all we can present
> Because of water pollution
> In the river Trent
> Because of water pollution, my boys,
> And a lack of concerted action,
> These fish of what they used to be
> Is only a measly fraction
> A-swimming about most roomily
> Where they shoved each other before,
> Yet not beefing about being solitary
> Or the sparseness of the fare . . . [3]

This glorious nonsense does bring us round again, after a fashion, to the theme of the earlier part of the chapter.

1. *Poems*, p. 367.
2. *Ibid.*, p. 563.
3. *Ibid.*, p. 472.

9

To Carry the Child

'The Poetic Genius is the true Man.' (Blake)

In unsophisticated communities, even today, everyday speech may be a kind of poetry. It has also been suggested that, in prehistory, song developed before speech as a means of communication. I believe that there is evidence that primitive or unsophisticated people, like animals, possess paranormal faculties, and that these become repressed with the advance of civilization. The first party of Tristan Islanders to return home, after their harbour and village had been restored, had no doubt at all that they were in telepathic touch with their fellow-islanders still in England.

Norman O. Brown, in *Life Against Death* has written . . . 'It is one of the great romantic visions, clearly formulated by Schiller and Herder as early as 1793 . . . that the history of mankind consists in a departure from a condition of undifferentiated primal unity with himself and with nature, an intermediate period in which man's powers are developed through differentiation and antagonism (alienation) . . . and a final return to a unity on a higher level of harmony'[1]. As with the race, so with the individual. Professor Brown believes that, in the child 'the conscious and the unconscious are not yet separated'. If anyone doubts the visionary nature of the child's experience let him look at the free art work of young children, who do no more than put on to paper what they see; but what they see is not what the average adult sees. Picasso remarked that a strong formative influence on the work of Matisse was the free painting of his children — the spontaneous naïvety of their work radically altered his direction. But unfortunately the cult of mathematical abstraction has taken over in many art classes in our schools — and who can estimate the consequent loss to the child? Poets, and artists in general, when uncorrupted, are those who have retained the unitive vision of childhood.

Thinkers as diverse as the heretical Christian mystic Jacob Boehme, the poet-philosopher Schiller, and the psychologist Freud have

---

1. Norman O. Brown, *Life Against Death*, (Middleton, U.S.A., 1959), Sphere (London), 1970, p. 83.

defined the essential human activity as play. To quote Professor Brown again: 'Boehme placed man's perfection and bliss not in a Protestant future life nor in Catholic sacraments but in the transformation of this bodily life into joyful play. Underneath the habit of work in every man lies the immortal instinct for play'. He goes on to say that, from the Freudian point of view, 'every ordinary man has tasted the paradise of play in his childhood'.[1]

Archie and Tina
Where are you now,
Playmates of my childhood,
Brother and sister?

When we stayed in the same place
With Archie and Tina
At the seaside,
We used

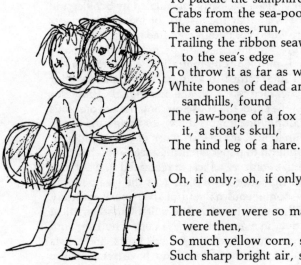

To paddle the samphire beds, fish
Crabs from the sea-pool, poke
The anemones, run,
Trailing the ribbon seaweed across the sand
   to the sea's edge
To throw it as far as we could. We dug
White bones of dead animals from the
   sandhills, found
The jaw-bone of a fox with some teeth in
   it, a stoat's skull,
The hind leg of a hare.

Oh, if only; oh, if only! . . .

There never were so many poppies as there
   were then,
So much yellow corn, so many fine days,
Such sharp bright air, such seas . . .

I remember
Such pleasure, so much pleasure.[2]

1. Brown, *Life Against Death* (1970), pp. 40–41.
2. *Poems*, p. 549.

The poet (and I here use the word as synonymous with artist) is one who has carried the child into adult life, as Stevie puts it; he has kept alive the child's sense of wonder. The play-element in poetry is expressed in metaphor, symbol, and the various devices of tone, rhyme and rhythm. The candid, wide-eyed vision of childhood and of feeling, thought and word which embody it, pervade Stevie's work, and occasionally, as with Carroll and Lear, emerges as pure play, either with an element of symbolism, as so often in the case of Lear, or as sheer, if significant-seeming nonsense:

> The Cock of the North
> And the Cock of the Fen
> Are one and the same,
> And one is the bane
> Of the Hen
> Of the Cock of the North and the Fen
> Who sits in a pen
> Of forgotten worth
> In a Fen in the North
> Woe for them both.[1]

Little more than word-play; yet it disturbs the unconscious mind, and seems to sound a note of apocalyptic warning.

In his study, *The Brontë Sisters*, Ernest Dimnet wrote of the change that takes place in the child at around the age of ten: 'The power with which the civilized world takes possession at this moment of the faculties of children results in a forcing upon them of artificial ways of seeing and feeling which only a few of them can resist'.[2] And though the artist has succeeded in resisting, and has retained something of the glory and spontaneity of childhood, he must, as Jung has remarked, and as Stevie for one experienced, pay dearly for the gift of creative fire. The price may be neurosis, or total breakdown; and there is often a streak of childishness, which can exist side-by-side with formidable intellectual power, and which is apt to break out unpredictably. One thinks of Mozart, of Shelley, of Lewis Carroll and of many more in this connection. As we have seen, Stevie felt that the child in adult life was defenceless:

> But oh the poor child, the poor child, what can he do,
> Trapped in a grown-up carapace,

1. *Poems*, p. 109, 'The Cock and the Hen'.
2. Ernest Dimnet, *The Brontë Sisters*, translated by Louise Morgan Sill, Jonathan Cape (London), 1927, p. 28.

But peer outside of his prison room
With the eye of an anarchist?[1]

And yet in the last resort, even if it had been possible, one cannot
imagine that she would have allowed the child in her to perish and
'the clever grown-up, the man-of-the-world, the frozen'[2] to take
over. In 'Parents' she showed the other side of the picture. The two
children have been sent, with the best intentions and considerable
self-sacrifice, to expensive boarding-schools. The son, an ordinary
likeable youth, is 'saved'; he has kept alive something of the child:

> . . . ponds, duck, fish in dark water
> Have a tight hold of him. It is your daughter
> Colonel, who is wholly corrupted.
> Women when they are snobbish do not loaf
> Look at fish, are not oafish
> But are persistently mercenary, cold, scheming
>   and calculating,
> This in a young girl is revolting . . . [3]

1. *Poems*, p. 437, 'To Carry the Child'.
2. *Ibid.*
3. *Ibid.*, p. 356.

And a similar thought is expressed delightfully in *The Holiday*. Celia exclaims: 'Oh leave it, leave it, you horrible fashion girl, be careless, lively, intelligent and dirty. I love grubby girls . . . with the hair in their eyes and the pastel-coloured features screwed in absurd concentration . . . The fashion slant is smug, careful, sly and witholding'.[1] Edward Lear would surely have recognized his Jumbly Girl in this passage.

1. *The Holiday*, 1949 and 1979, p. 123

10

A Wrestling Power

With few exceptions creative artists, whether or not they subscribe to any particular creed, share a profoundly religious attitude to life. They cannot but feel that their vision, and the forces which possess them in the act of creation, are related to the ultimate nature of reality and come from a region not accessible to pure reason. Coleridge declared: 'The primary imagination I hold to be the living power and prime agent of all human perception, and as a repetition in the finite mind of the eternal act of creation in the infinite I AM'. The conceptions of mechanistic psychology are felt by the artist, if he bothers to think about them at all, to deny the validity of his experience, for he cannot doubt his vision. Blake sang it succinctly in a quatrain from *Auguries of Innocence*:

> He who Doubts from what he sees
> Will ne'er Believe, do what you Please.
> If the Sun and Moon should doubt,
> They'd immediately Go out.

Were the artist to question the report of his inner eye, which in fact he cannot, the vision would dissolve.

The intensity of passion with which the mechanistic, reductionist psychologist or philosopher challenges the existence of intrinsic values may sometimes be the measure of his own repressed religious feeling, and it also, I am sure, betrays his panic at the thought that his beliefs are under threat; for a belief is usually an emotional vested interest to with the believer will cling for dear life. It is unfortunate that the English language has only one word 'knowledge' to express quite diverse modes of knowing. It should, I think, be obvious that logical, rational knowledge is knowledge about, not of, certain orders of experience. These are known by intimate acquaintance, by intuitional, or, as I would prefer to call it, empathic knowledge, which can never be replaced by reasoning. It is surely a pity that Professor James, in his illuminating book from which I quoted earlier, is ready to abandon the word 'knowledge' to the rationalists, the reason being presumably that, as a believing Christian, he takes his stand on *faith*.

I owe an apology to those readers who may feel that such philosophising is out-of-place here. There are also those, who, while sympathetically inclined to Stevie's work in general, do not realise how central a place religion holds in her poetic world. Mr. James MacGibbon is clearly not among them for, in editing the *Collected Poems*, he has placed the poem 'Mr. Over':

> And who pray is this You
> To whom Mr. Over is gone? . . . [1]

inside the flap of the dust-jacket.

1. *Poems*, p. 262.

Stevie's first serious attempt to explore the religious consciousness is found in the poem 'Mother, among the Dustbins'. It consists of a dialogue between a mystically attuned girl and her mother who, though she conceded:

> I too have felt the presence of God in the broom
> I hold, in the cobwebs in the room,
> But most of all in the silence of the tomb . . . [1]

remains gravely sceptical. Yet I think that Stevie has given the girl, in her pert reply, the final say in the matter. Scepticism has been allowed to have a say in other poems, for example in 'Will Man Ever Face Fact and not Feel Flat?'

> But then came a little wind sneaking along
> That was older than all and infamously strong,
> 'Oh what an artistic animal is our little Man',
> Sneered the wind, 'It is wonderful how he can
> Invent fairy stories about everything, pit pat,
> Will he ever face fact and not feel flat?'[2]

But Stevie, feeling her way by thesis and antithesis, must be allowed to contradict herself. In her fourth volume of poems, and in her novel *The Holiday*, written not long before, she expressed a positive religious insight. Jacob Boehme affirmed that 'The Being of all beings is a wrestling power', and Blake expressed a similar conception in his famous engraving 'God creating Adam', where the Deity is depicted as bending over man, moulding him with infinite love and care into the Divine image. Man, in Stevie's thought, as in that of Boehme and Blake, is the delicate growing-point of creation. He may succeed in 'coming out of the mountains' (to quote another of Stevie's poems), or also he may all too easily perish: it is as she says, 'touch and go',[3] and in another poem 'God and Man', the creative force, in its higher reaches, is shown as visionary sculptor:

> In man is my life, and in man is my death,
> He is my hazard, my pride and my breath,
> I sought him, I wrought him, I pant on his worth,
> In him I experience indeterminate growth . . .

1. *Poems*, p. 118.
2. *Ibid.*, p. 341.
3. *Ibid.*, p. 235.

The poem ends with a faltering cadence of great beauty:

> Oh Man, Man, of all my animals dearest,
> Do not come till I call, though thou weariest first.[1]

In these final lines (as in the opening stanza which I have not quoted) Man is crowned, as it were, by the capital 'M', which seems to suggest that he is achieving, or capable of achieving, his divine potential. There is an old Hindu saying to the effect that if God wished to hide, he would choose a man to hide in. The small 'm' is for man as merely generic so to speak. Stevie gave much thought to capitals — when to employ them and when not — just as she did to punctuation.

In a later poem 'God Speaks' the poet adds another touch to her account of God's purpose with man:

> All the same, there is a difficulty. I should like him to be happy in heaven here,
> But he cannot come by wishing. Only by being already at home here.[2]

J. B. Priestley has dramatized the same idea in his beautiful play *They Came to a City*. Some of his characters, on entering the City, felt immediately at home; others felt so ill-at-ease that they made haste to depart.

In these poems, Stevie sees humanity as material with which the visionary part of the creative force is working to release latent divinity, much as the light seeks, as it were, to penetrate an opaque or muddied pane of glass. She sees a deity fully aware and sure of his goal. But on one occasion in 'Thoughts about the Person from Porlock', she sees him as an artist, trying out on his canvas various relations of form and colour or, more disturbingly still, as a coolly detached scientific experimenter:

> . . . we should smile as well as submitting
> To the purpose of One Above who is experimenting
> With various mixtures of human character which goes best . . . [3]

This idea of a power uncertain of its direction was, I would like to think, no more than a passing misgiving: on the other hand she did

1. *Poems*, p. 261.
2. *Ibid.*, p. 403.
3. *Ibid.*, p. 386.

give the poem emphasis by placing it first in the volume.

Stevie's religious poems are, of course, symbolic visions rather than arguments, and she is not to be pinned down to any of them. Yet there is on the whole a general direction in her thought, a prevailing wind as it were: the creative force, in its higher reaches at least, is seen as benign, and as knowing what it is about. There is no suggestion that God is responsible for the evil in creation; I think that the implication is that he is not omnipotent and cannot force man to do his will, or abolish evil at a stroke. The struggle, however painful, has to go on — that is the nature of things. Man

is pigment, canvas, marble to be used, but only with his co-operation, to realize a vision, Blake's 'Divine Humanity', whether, after death, he persists as an individual entity, with the richness gained from experience of good and evil, sadness and joy, or whether he is to be absorbed, together with all his experience, into the Whole.

In *The Holiday* Stevie described the drama in somewhat different terms:

> . . . 'I think that man is composed of three things. There is the man . . . and the cards he is playing, and there is a man watching over his shoulder . . .
> . . . And the cards are the fate, and the player is the life, and the watcher is the spirit. Yes, this Watcher is a bit of an enigma. Perhaps he is the *Weltgeist*. So then it is like a dream, it shifts, and the player and the cards vanish, but in their place there is now a stream that is made of two parts, that mix together, that make a food mixture. But the spirit is there, and he is hungry' . . . [1]

If I understand this rightly, she is saying that the person is dealt certain cards, 'lucky' or 'unlucky', by fate, which may not be mere chance. Her 'food mixture' is the interaction of the player and his destiny. The spirit, and his appetite, is surely the magnet or catalyst determining the whole process.

Stevie returned to this theme in later poems, in 'Childe Rolandine'[2] and especially in 'God the Eater':

1. *The Holiday*, 1949 and 1979, pp. 49–50.
2. *Poems*, p. 331.

There is a god in whom I do not believe
Yet to this god my love stretches,
This god whom I do not believe in is
My whole life, my life and I am his.

How better than by this paradoxical utterance to express a religious intuition, tempered by agnostic caution? The poem continues:

Everything that I have of pleasure and pain
(Of pain, of bitter pain and men's contempt)
I give this god for him to feed upon
As he is my whole life and I am his.

When I am dead I hope he will eat
Everything I have been and have not been
And crunch and feed upon it and grow fat
Eating my life all up as it is his.[1]

These strange poems are surely among the most honest, searching and subtle of their kind in the language.

1. *Poems*, p. 339.

11

To Fatness Come

'The Queen and the Young Princess' is a dialogue between mother and daughter. The Queen, the mature personality (the crown is, I think, a symbol of full human stature), may possibly be the Lion Aunt, and the girl, Stevie herself. The Princess wonders what she can expect from life, and the Queen replies that it will be much the same as it has been for her. Says the child:

> But Mother you often say you
>   have a headache
> Because of the crown you wear
>   for duty's sake.

to which the mother replies:

> So it is, so it is, a headache I have
> And that is what you must grow
>   up to carry to the grave . . .

The child asks whether there are not delights to alleviate the burden of living, 'the pleasant weather . . . the bluebottle and the soft feather', but the mother sums up gravely:

> Ah my child, that joy you speak of must be a pleasure
> Of human stature, not the measure
> Of animals, who have no glorious duty
> To perform, no headache and so cannot see beauty.
> Up, child, up, embrace the headache and the crown
> Marred pleasure's best, shadow makes the sun strong.[1]

1. *Poems*, p. 313.

I feel that 'shadow makes the sun strong' is not universally true. The child needs no shadow to enhance its delight in living and, incidentally, the Buddhist religion avers that Nirvana is a state of undiluted bliss. That household pest the bluebottle seems an odd choice for a symbol of life's delights until one recalls his opalescence. In *Novel on Yellow Paper* she writes: 'The thing that really counts is what is making you all the time, and forming you into being the sort of definite person that, clear as if it was labelled, has its own place to go to. And what is so important is what you are selecting all the time and discarding as the years go on, making yourself into this sort of a very definite person, with his own place to go to'.[1]

At this point I ought, perhaps, to apologize in advance for a rather long divagation. Stevie's recurring preoccupation with the purpose of life and the destiny of mankind form so substantial a part of her work that I feel they should be seen in relation to the thinking of other poet-philosophers. Commenting on Keats' famous letter concerning what he described as 'soul-making', Professor D. G. James wrote with beautiful clarity: 'Keats' idea appears to be that the world affords opportunity to the bare, pure identitiy of the child to evolve into individuality and self-possession — a process only possible through pain and suffering. The soul which is finally brought into being has the wholeness and perfection of the child, but combines such wholeness with a sense of identity and individual being: the soul at this level becomes 'God' again, though at a higher level of creation than the 'intelligence' of the child'.[2] Keats' conception, as Professor James notes, involves the assumption that the soul survives after death. The growth to divine stature necessitates continuity; otherwise there would be no ultimate gain in learning through the trials of experience. Blake expressed the same conception: Innocence, leading through Experience, to full humanity, which he called Imagination and, in his later work, Jerusalem. 'Imagination' he declared, 'is not a State, it is the Human Existence itself'. The definite article is vital here — 'Imagination' is the specifically human existence, the ultimate goal of the Creative Force.

Keats also declared that 'A Man's life of any worth is a continual allegory, and very few eyes can see the mystery of his life . . . a life, like the scriptures, figurative'. To some people, such words will appear to be no more than fanciful speculation; to others, as the years pass, they will increasingly ring true. But how could a mere youth, with so brief an experience of living, attain to such insight? Keats went on to say: 'Shakespeare led a life of allegory: his words

1. *Novel on Yellow Paper*, p. 183.
2. David G. James, *Scepticism & Poetry* (1937), p. 203.

are a comment on it', So it was largely through his study of Shakespeare, of the symbolic pattern unfolded in his work, that Keats achieved this understanding.

The conception of life as a continual allegory has been approached from another angle by the Northern Irish mystic AE (George Russell) who, in *The Candle of Vision*, wrote of what he described as a 'law of spiritual gravitation, like that which in the chemistry of nature makes one molecule fly to another', and by which we draw to ourselves events, circumstances, persons, ideas. 'I remember' he continued, 'the exultation with which I realized about life that, as Heraclitus has said, it was in a flux, and that in all its flowings there was meaning and law . . . I need not seek, for what was my own would come to me; if any passed it was because they were no longer mine'.[1] Stevie herself felt that we must flow with the current, which is something quite different from mere drifting, and we must try to sense its direction. She quotes the Latin proverb *Fata nolentem trahunt, volentem ducunt* (the fates drag the unwilling, the willing they lead). A few lines later AE continues: 'It is those who live and grow swiftly, and who continually compare what is without with what is within, who have this certainty. Those who do not change see no change and recognize no law.'[2] Of course I am not assuming that Stevie had precisely this kind or experience, but I think that there are indications in her writing that she did. Her symbolic picture of human existence, quoted in Chapter 10, of the player, the cards and the watcher, is not far removed from Keats's idea of life as a continual allegory.

'The Frog Prince' gives its title to Stevie's penultimate volume and her placing it first gives, as usual, special emphasis to it. The theme is that of rebirth. The spellbound frog has barely tasted the rigours of Experience, he resembles those people, in 'The Crown of Bays'

. . . in deep slumbers
Who travel in the Underground railway
with happy faces in numbers . . . [3]

1. G. W. Russell (pseud. A.E), *The Candle of Vision* (Macmillan, London, 1918), Quest (Illinois), 1974, p. 17.
2. *Ibid.*
3. *Poems*, p. 276.

But he feels stirrings of divine discontent: a thought comes to him and says:

It is part of the spell
To be happy . . .
To fear
    disenchantment . . .
Says, it will be *heavenly*
To be set free,
Cries, *Heavenly* the girl who
    disenchants
And the royal times, *heavenly*,
And I think it will be.

Come then, royal girl and royal
    times,
Come quickly,
I can be happy until you come
But I cannot be heavenly,
Only disenchanted people
Can be heavenly.[1]

The fairy tale is of course, like fairy tales in general, an archetypal myth: its theme is the urge towards self-completion and fulfilment — the quest for the *anima* figure to consummate union in the Divine Androgyne. Disillusionment — Blake's 'Experience', the Queen's 'headache', — is the inescapable price to be paid. But there is drastic compression in this account: the long duress of 'headache' is, so to speak, leap-frogged.

As we saw earlier, Stevie found, when comparatively young, that fulfilment in love was not to be her lot. It may be, perhaps, that she regarded poetic creation as an alternative to a full life, as *faute de mieux*, a poor second-best ('When I am happy I live and despise writing'). She certainly came to realise, as AE did, that what was truly her own would come to her, and that a deep love-relationship was not part of her destiny. The lovely poem 'Votaries of Both Sexes Cry First to Venus' is again relevant. One of the votaries offers his passionate feelings to the goddess of love, but in vain; he finds he must turn elsewhere. The theme is not simply of sublimation, but also, as in 'The Frog Prince', of Rebirth:

1. *Poems*, p. 407.

> . . . on the soft dark grass I lay down
> My strong feelings. They are for you to eat up, Venus
> But you do not care for them much. Then they are
> For the god who created me. Let him have them.
>
> Then this person began to laugh and to dance
> And Venus was offended; but behind Venus there came
> First a little light, then some laughter, then a hand
> That took up the great feelings, and then a blessing fell
> Like the moon, and there was not Venus any longer
> But the votaries were not abashed, they were blessed . . . [1]

So is the bitterness of sacrifice turned to sweetness. 'First a little light, then some laughter'. Laughter for joy is revealed, once again, as an attribute of deity. There is great tenderness in these long fluctuating lines, and the metre is handled with consummate grace.

Stevie's last and most touching word on man's thorny road to fulfilment is found in one of her very late poems, 'So to fatness come:'

> Poor human race that must
> Feed on pain, or choose another dish
> And hunger worse . . .
>
> I am thy friend, I wish
> You to sup full of the dish
> I give you and the drink,
> And so to fatness come more than you think
> In health of opened heart, and know peace.
>
> Grief spake these words to me in a dream, I thought
> He spoke no more than grace allowed
> And no less than truth. [2]

It is surely a 'heavenly' voice that speaks in these poems. One would like to think that the concluding lines indicate that Stevie's tormented spirit had at last come to rest after her long pilgrimage.

---

1. *Poems*, pp. 399–400.
2. *Ibid.*, p. 538.

12

Fear is a Band of Gold

It need hardly be said that no poetry of any profundity yields all
its secrets on first acquaintance. Some poets take longer to know
intimately than others, and the same applies to individual poems.
I have found, in becoming more familiar with the unique poetic
individuality that was Stevie Smith, that certain poems which did
not at first especially interest me later disclosed a beauty which I
had not suspected, and that even those that had made an immediate
impact revealed, on returning to them, a deeper level of significance
than I had perceived originally. The same applies to the novels.

In the opening chapter I wrote of the strange quality of Stevie's
imagination, conveyed by a brilliantly idiosyncratic poetic diction,
and also suggested that her work extended over a far wider range
than had been generally recognized, and that it would be a mistake
to relegate her to the position of a minor poet. In Chapter two I
attempted to justify this high evaluation by placing one of her poems,
though without making extravagant claims for it, alongside some
lines from what some consider to be Coleridge's greatest poem.

I am well aware that excessive eulogy would be self-defeating; but
I do suspect that the critical establishment in general, having made
a conscientious attempt to assess her work, now feels that it has found
a niche for her among the foothills of Parnassus, and that justice
has been done. If, as I feel, it has not yet been done except by a
small minority of critics, this may be due in part to the present-day
climate, and to current fashions, in the arts in general and in poetry
in particular. There is a widespread inhibiting attitude both to
romance and to visionary experience, together with the idea that the
poetic tradition with has held sway through the centuries is
exhausted, and that a fresh start must be made on more modest lines.
It is felt that we are now grown-up, or ought to be, and must dispense
with poetic dreaming. Such a negative attitude is surely unfavourable
to the conditions in which vital poetry can emerge.

In this and in Chapter 14 I propose to look more closely at the
musical and magical qualities in Stevie Smith's work. These are
shown in her lyrical poems, and also in the fairy tales, or what might

be termed the legendary poems. These last, together with the dramatic ballads, are the subject of this chapter, and contain some of her highest flights of imagination.

Poems concerning enticement or captivity, such as 'The Warden' and 'The River God',[1] present no difficulty; the latter in particular is ripe for anthologies. A highly idiosyncratic poem 'The Magic Morning', on the ancient theme of the Lorelei, may be found too mannered by some readers. It is a romantic but sinister tale, illustrated by one of her finest drawings. There are some lines of impressionist nature-painting:

> . . . he rowed her upon the lake.
> He rowed her across the lake until the green shallows
> Paled in a waxen lily litter striped with swallows.
> And now the morning sun flecks the dark trees
> And lightly the mauve sedge moves in a little breeze . . .

The collapse into banal verbiage is a device which is all her own:

> 'Never more', cries the swan, 'shall Charley be seen,
> He is underneath the water of the mis-en-scène,'
> (And 'Charley, Charley, Charley' cry the swan-instructed curlews
> Ever after as they fly to their nests in the purlieus) . . . [2]

1. *Poems*, pp. 232 and 238.
2. *Ibid.*, pp. 205–6.

Often the charm of these poems lies as much in their shaping, in line and stanza, as in their imagery. 'The Castle'[1] is not a nonsense poem, nor can it be described as surrealist, but as Celia said of it in *The Holiday*, 'It is not sensible'. It is pure romance. A longer and even more mysterious ballad is 'The Frozen Lake'. It would be fruitless to ask what is the connection between Lord Ullan's daughter, who has become

> . . . a witch of endless might
> And rules the borders of the night . . .

and Arthurian legend, represented by Sir Bedivere and the Sword Excalibur. Stevie's only comment, in the deleted 'Listen' recording, was to say that the poem showed 'the danger of traffic with the fairy wood'. One enjoys it as one enjoys, say, a Ballade by Chopin, sensing a latent significance but without looking for a programme:

> No, this water is not vacant
> But is full of deep intent
> Of deep intent and management
> Contrived by Ullan's daughter
> To what end I know not.
>
> And to my mind the lake is brighter
> For the Lady's presence; whiter
> Though its coat of winter make it
> It is for Ullan's daughter's sake it
> Beams to me so brightly . . .[2]

'The Blue from Heaven; A legend of King Arthur of Britain, with yet another exquisite drawing, is more readily understood. We know that the legendary Arthur suffered from a strange sickness; apart from that we must put aside all thought of Mallory or Tennyson. What has taken possession of Arthur here is the quest of ideal beauty, with an indifference to all human ties and royal responsibilites:

> All I wish for now, said Arthur,
> Is the beautiful colour blue
> And to ride in the blue sunshine
> And Guinevere I do not wish for you . . .

And the poem concludes:

1. *Poems*, p. 228.
2. *Ibid.*, pp. 393–4.

Yes, Arthur has passed away
Gladly he has laid down his reigning powers
He has gone to ride in the blue light
Of the peculiar towering cornflowers.[1]

These strange poems may not, on first acquaintance, fully disclose
their spell, which is achieved largely by subtle irregularities of form
and metre. They leave a singing in the mind, and I think, call for
musical setting — one can almost hear the harmony and
instrumentation.

I have left till last two dramatic poems 'Eulenspiegelei' and 'Songe
d'Athalie', in which Stevie's 'word of fear' strikes a note of high
tragedy. This Eulenspeigel is a creature of an incomparably darker
order than the mischievous rogue of German folklore: he symbolizes
the burgeoning evil in the heart of a child. The drawing depicts an
attic room with sloping roof and uncurtained window, and adds a
further dimension to the poem. The storm without mirrors the storm
within the room. On the bed the mother, wide-eyed with terror,
strives to hold back the infant girl who is riven by conflict:

To be so cold and yet not old
Oh what can ail the changeling child?

1. *Poems*, pp. 309–10.

She has an eye that is too bold
Upon the night. She is beguiled.

The night is dark and the windowpane
Holds the rattle of the falling rain.
Oh look not out but look within
Where the room lies safe from the stormwinds' din . . .

The tension mounts until the demon within the child has accomplished his purpose:

Oh whither is fled thy
   changeling child
And by what witching craft?
It was the Eulenspiegel spake
And as he spake he laughed.

For well he knew that
   wrought it so,
The bitch and the changeling
   too
Are vanished away from the
   stormwinds' play
And the stricken mother's
   mew.[1]

It would be easy to underestimate this idiosyncratic poem. Without attempting to set it on a level with Goethe's tremendous Erl-King, the parallel cannot be missed. In Stevie's poem it is the survival not merely of a life but of a soul that is at stake.

In 'Songe d'Athalie (From Racine)' the narrator is the daughter of Queen Jezebel. From the Old Testament story we are familiar with the Hebrew point of view, but Racine, whom Stevie greatly admired, shows us the other side of the picture. The poem is one of her essays in free verse which she handles with consummate ease and controlled metrical fluidity. The poem builds up from a restrained opening to a shattering climax:

It was a dream and shouldn't I bother about a dream?
But it goes on you know, tears me rather.
Of course I try to forget it but it will not let me.

1. *Poems*, pp. 98–9.

Well it was on an extraordinarily dark night at midnight
My mother Queen Jezebel appeared suddenly before me
Looking just as she did the day she died, dressed grandly.
It was her pride you noticed, nothing she had gone through
touched that
And she still had the look of being most carefully made up
She always made up a lot she didn't want people to know how
old she was.
She spoke: Be warned my daughter, true girl to me, she said,
Do not suppose the cruel God of the Jews has finished with you,
I am come to weep your falling into his hands, my child.
With these appalling words my mother,
This ghost, leant over me stretching out her hands
And I stretched out my hands too to touch her
But what was it, oh this is horrible, what did I touch?
Nothing but the mangled flesh and the breaking bones
Of a body that the dogs tearing quarrelled over.[1]

These two poems live in the realm of pity and terror, and I submit
that they are small tragic masterpeices.

1. *Poems*, p. 324.

13

Fun and Games

'Oh why was I born with a different face?' (Blake)

The philosopher Bergson demonstrated — though it scarcely needed demonstration — that wherever there is humour we are aware of the incongruous. Incongruity pervades Stevie Smith's work, both in the poems and the three novels. Along with Carroll and Lear in English poetry she has carried the sense of the ludicrous to an extreme. In the work of Carroll — whom I would not exclude from the company of poets, he is surely poetical in essence — there is always the sense of dreaming. Alice moves in a world of automata not without human traits; and we know that she will shortly wake up. I think that Lear, the more lyrical of the two, but equally fantastic and dreamlike, is in essence subtly nearer to actuality, and consequently there is in his work a greater awareness of the tragic sense of life. In both these poets there is a strong element of sadism, although Lear was one of the kindliest of men. According to a recent study, a good deal of nastiness was hidden in his woodshed — and I am speaking of more than the evident and innocuous Freudian symbolism. But the saving clause is that he kept it there.

It is plain that, like Stevie, Carroll and Lear had suffered grievous damage. Carroll was I think, the weaker of the two, in the last resort more vulnerable than Lear. His genius succumbed early to neurosis and to the pressure of the Victorian ambience. In Lear, severe physical ailments produced a tendency to deep melancholia. But in Stevie's work there is an absence of repression and disguise, together with a rare degree of mental honesty and self-knowledge. Of sadism there is only a hint and, as has been said earlier, she abominated cruelty. In the poem 'Seymour and Chantelle',[1] painful reading though it is, she displays a clinical detachment. This is borne out by her remarks on Swinburne and Mary Gordon in a review in *Me Again*.[2] And of course Lear was not overborne by his melancholy: he sometimes wrote poems of unalloyed delight. Such are 'The

---

1. *Poems*, p. 514.
2. Stevie Smith, *Me Again, Uncollected Writings of Stevie Smith: Illustrated by Herself*, Virago (London), 1981, pp. 187–191.

Pelican Chorus' and 'The Table and the Chair': incidentally the latter has been set to music ideally by Victor Hely-Hutchinson in his trio of Lear settings. This is a tiny gem of tenderness which should not be allowed to perish. It is strange that Lear's verse has not often, to my knowledge, been set memorably. Several composers have tried their hands at setting Stevie's poems, but oddly enough they have generally passed by those which seem to cry out for musical setting.

I think one could say that where Carroll dreams, and Lear is usually at least half-awake, Stevie is fully conscious and keeps one foot on the ground. Lear's is a world painted in exotic verbal colours. Carroll has his own distorted logic — he was a mathematician. Lear created a vivid landscape with its strange flora and fauna, in which sense is overthrown. One suspects that he and Henri Rousseau would have got along together very nicely. Stevie's world is very different, and despite all its idiosyncracies is recognisably our own. And while Carroll does not evoke musical feeling, both Lear and Stevie Smith are replete with verbal and pictorial music. In Carroll, pain and suffering are distanced, muted by the dream-like atmosphere. His oysters, so cruelly led up the garden path, are an exception, they are real enough to elicit a pang of sympathy. In Lear and Stevie pain and suffering are often vividly present.

Central themes of Romanticism pervade Stevie's work as we have seen: alienation, the Outsider, the innocent eye of childhood, the 'Heaven and Hell' of Blake. It is here, and in her hatred of mediocrity, that she has so much in common with Lear. Lear's verse was widely enjoyed by his contemporaries. He was perhaps seen principally as the producer of wildly dotty rhymes for the young, which adults might also, without loss of dignity, stoop a little to enjoy. But this very wildness acted, I think, as a safety valve for the repressed emotions of the staid and outwardly puritanical Victorians. It has been said that the English and the French are the only two peoples which gladly tolerate eccentricity. The French have produced some notable eccentrics. Yet oddly enough the late and much lamented Jacques Tati declared that his films were more highly appreciated in England than in his native France. One fears that these cardinal virtues, tolerance and even delight in eccentricity, may in our age be gradually eroded by industrialism and hypertrophied technology, with their resultant grey cloud of uniformity and vulgarity, and in the arts by the pseudo-aesthetics of Karl Marx. But, as Herbert Read suggested, what passes for normality in our society may simply be the commonest form of neurosis.

'. . . very narrow little minds . . . these people have . . . They

turn away from the sunshine, they are strong to come together
to oppose every great idea that is . . . coming forth with blood
and tears brought to birth they will beat it down and tread it down
. . into the ground.

Oh I know them very well they are as cruel as sin more cruel
than death . . . *Insuffisance*, defeatism an incorruptible fidelity
to the worse and the lower . . . Apostles of the inferior, evangels
of the All-Lowest, *oh royaume des aveugles!*'[1]

The work of Lear, and in large part that of Stevie, contain a defiant
exaltation of non-conformity, together with a contempt for the abject
fear of not going along with the crowd, or of following prevailing
trends. Stevie never gave a thought to current fashions:

'My dear, how can we tell that nice Mrs. Snooks? Why she still
washes her face the old way! Won't anybody tell her she'll never
get a partner while she talks about El Greco?'[2]

And from Lear:

> They went to sea in a Sieve, they did
> In a Sieve they went to sea:
> In spite of all their friends could say,
> On a winter's morn, on a stormy day,
> In a Sieve they went to sea!
>
> And when the Sieve turned round and round,
> And when everyone cried 'You'll all be drowned!'
> They called aloud, 'Our Sieve ain't big,
> But we don't care a button, we don't care a fig!
> In a Sieve we'll go to sea! . . .'

The recurrent motif of Lear's limericks is the humiliation and
occasional liquidation of the non-conformer. Many of his eccentrics
suffer from ostracism:

> There was an Old Man of Thermopylae
> Who never did anything properly,
>   But they said 'If you choose
>   To boil eggs in your shoes
> You shall never remain in Thermopylae'.

Others such as 'The Old Man of Whitehaven' suffered a far crueller

1. *Novel on Yellow Paper*, 1936 and 1980, pp. 219–20.
2. *Ibid.*, pp. 117–8.

fate; perhaps it may not be too far-fetched to see 'The Old Man with a Beard's' profuse hirsute growth as the poet's creative productivity, and the avian colony as the price he had to pay for it. The burden is borne with resignation. And likewise:

> There was a Young Lady whose bonnet
> Came untied when the birds sat upon it;
> But she said 'I don't care!
> All the birds of the air
> Are welcome to sit on my bonnet!'

The theme is similar, and again there is the note of defiance. I cannot resist the temptation of seeing here a pre-view of Stevie herself, bearing in mind the remarkable hats depicted in several of her drawings which seem to signify the luxuriance of her poetic creation. The poem 'My Hat' depicts a young woman flying through the air borne up by an enormous hat furnished with swan's wings. She has been carried away to a desert island:

> This hat being so strong has completely run away with me
> I had the feeling it was beginning to happen the moment I put it on
> What a moment that was as I rose up, I rose up like a flying swan
> As strong as a swan too, why see how far my hat has flown me away
> It took us a night to come here and then a night and a day . . .
> Am I glad to be here? Yes, well I am,
> It's nice to be rid of Father, Mother and the young man

There's just one thing causes me a twinge of pain
If I take my hat off, shall I find myself at home again?
So in this early morning land I always wear my hat
Go home, you see, well I wouldn't run a risk like that.[1]

In the grip of inspiration she is transported, indifferent to all else.
And in 'Magna est Veritas'[2] the poet describes her tall hat as 'rather
a temple'.

The mediocrity which Stevie and Lear feared and despised is a
condition of sub-humanity — man degraded to the level of an
automaton. Her most biting specimen of the mediocre is 'The Face'
which I have quoted earlier. The artist is surely entitled to pride in

1. *Poems*, p. 315.
2. *Ibid.*, p. 372.

his work, like any skilled or gifted professional. 'The pride of the peacock is the glory of God', as Blake had it. 'There is nothing so superior as false humility' wrote Stevie in *Novel on Yellow Paper*. Yet I see no lack of true humility in Stevie, or in Lear with his endearing self-mockery. Stevie loved and respected the good wholemeal bread of common, untainted humanity, while spurning the packaged and sliced loaf. 'This is a world of ignoble animals, and the noble animals are hated by the ignoble, and are killed by them, or suffer afflictions . . . And of course it is better to be noble and afflicted, in fact one can't help feeling sorry for the ignoble ones'.[1]

Stevie's aunt was the great and lasting love of her life. 'This lion has a very managing disposition, is strong, passionate, affectionate, has enormous moral strength, is a fine old Fielding creation[2] . . . Oh how deeply thankful I am that I didn't go having an aunt with clever ideas about literature and painting'.[3] And '. . . you must have an anchorage, someone that is fine and honest and strong . . . Oh what a fool I think Prunella was when she said to me: 'You want to get right away from that old-fashioned aunt of yours, Pompey, or you will find her an awful handicap, and your friends will laugh at you. It is not at all *chic* to live in a suburb with an aunt,' but my friends think she is looking like a lion and that is that'.[4] It is doubtful whether Stevie would have survived without her aunt. Such *positive* ordinariness transcends mediocrity. Great nobility of character is as rare and distinguished as creative originality, and it, too, can isolate as well as arouse envy and destructiveness in the mediocre.

'The Sliding Mountain' concerns a family immured in their own personal affairs, blind to the larger issues of life and totally unaware of what may be in store for them:

> The terrors of the scenery,
> The black rocks of the sliding mountain,
> Are hid from the man of family
> Who lives beneath the fountain.
> His name is Domesticity,
> He's married to an ivy tree,
> And the little children laugh and scream,
> For they do not know what these things mean.[5]

1. *Novel on Yellow Paper*, 1936 and 1980, pp. 68–9.
2. *Ibid.*, pp. 76–7.
3. *Ibid.*, p. 116.
4. *Ibid.*, p. 65.
5. *Poems*, p. 219.

This is somewhat reminiscent of Lear's Mr. and Mrs. Discobbolos, living on their wall in full view of the world, 'By all admired and by some respected', having, so they feel, nothing to hide. Their end is catastrophic, as will be the end of the family in Stevie's poem. Both are almost solely concerned with their own limited world — it is such who are examples of what Stevie means by the mediocre.

Wit, humour and verbal play pervade Stevie's work, whether in verse or in prose. One is hard put to define their essential qualities. It is not only what she says but her unique and inimitable way of saying it. There are satire, irony, (sometimes gentle, sometimes biting), her often eccentric rhyming, the odd, startling or prosy word and her passages of zany anti-climax:

> There was a loud crash from outside and Captain Maulay came bounding into the room with a paper bag full of cream buns . . . [1]

Finally there is her trick of deflation, the sudden lapses into trite banality, as in 'The Magic Morning'[2]. 'Lady Rogue' Singleton' is not in the least tempted by her suitor's ideal of life in Edmonton. She has quite other ideas for herself. Two of the poem's three stanzas collapse into banal verbiage, a device in which Stevie excels:

> I could never make you happy, darling,
> Or give you the baby you want,

1. *The Holiday*, 1949 and 1979, p. 15.
2. *Poems*, pp. 205–206.

> I would always very much rather, dear,
> Live in a tent.
>
> I am not a cold woman, Henry,
> But I do not feel for you,
> What I feel for the elephants and the miasmas
> And the general view.[1]

The comical drawing, which is missing from *The Collected Poems*,
shows the rogue elephant impatiently prodding the lady with his
tusks.

There is an episode in her sister Mary's life as a school teacher:

> My sister was not always so happy in her schools. In her last
> school, it was in Wales, it was like a mad-house. There it was
> a mixed boy-girl school, with a young, diffident and obstinate
> headmaster. He thought that to do the wrong thing strongly is
> better than to do nothing, but only he was by nature so vacillating
> that he could not even make up his mind what was the wrong
> thing, but if he was not impeded by a rationalizing attempt, he
> would do the wrong thing with a splendid spontaneity.[2]

But her humour is often shot through with irony, pathos or serious
intent. Poems of pure fun such as 'Friends of the River Trent' quoted
earlier are rather rare. The 'House of Over-Dew', a versified short
story about the obsessional Mr. Minnim and his family, is both sad
and at the same time comical. Mr. Minnim, 'a sincere and practising
Christian', harbours 'a dear wish' to move from the suburb where
they have been living and to buy a house in the country, 'A retreat
for missionaries to live/On their leave-taking holidays in England'.
Moving in winter they settle into the house:

> The House of Over-Dew
> Lay buried half in snow,
> It stood five miles from any town upon a hillside.
> Very bleak it was, and all the pipes were froze . . .
> . . .Mr Minnim
> Bought chasubles for visiting priests. But at first
> There were no visitors at all, but only
> The old cold house, and the lavatories frozen up . . .
> The work was bitter hard . . .

1. *Poems*, p. 194. It is illustrated in *Selected Poems*, p. 79.
2. *The Holiday*, 1949 and 1979, p. 58.

Mr. Minnim, released suddenly
From the routine of his accountancy
Suffered in his head a strange numbness,
He moved about in a dream, would take no hand with
   the dishes. Even
When twenty-five missionaries came for a conference
He would do nothing.
He paced the garden plot, 'And here', he said,
'I will build twelve lavatories. And in this room
We will have a consecration and build an altar . . . '[1]

1. *Poems*, pp. 557–8.

I suspect that this distressing, ludicrous, but by no means improbable story may have some foundation in fact.

'I Remember' is probably one of Stevie's best-known poems: it has been set, along with others, for A-level examinations. A little masterpiece of compression, it displays some of her favourite gambits such as some wildly erratic rhymes, and long straggling lines, mixed with short ones:

> It was my bridal night I remember,
> An old man of seventy-three
> I lay with my young bride in my arms,
> A girl with t.b.
> It was wartime, and overhead
> The Germans were making a particularly heavy raid on Hampstead.
> What rendered the confusion worse, perversely
> Our bombers had chosen that moment to set out for Germany.
> Harry, do they ever collide?
> I do not think it has ever happened.
> Oh my bride, my bride.[1]

This astonishing combination of the grotesque, and verbal high jinks, with pathos ends in a poignant last line. A. Alvarez gives this poem special mention in the review aptly entitled 'Deadly Funny' to which I have already referred in Chapter One.

In the 'Listen' recording, Stevie remarked that 'Life bears hard upon the children in these poems', and she went on to read 'If I lie down':

> If I lie down upon my bed I must be here,
> But if I lie down in my grave I may be elsewhere.[2]

What has befallen this little boy to cause him to harbour such thoughts? He is already among the lost ones. A child's spirit may be maimed not only by harsh treatment, by neglect or by owner-

1. *Poems*, p. 336.
2. *Ibid.*, p. 176.

anxious parents, but also by morbid or sadistic literature, religious or otherwise. The pathetic child in 'Louise' is victimized by selfishness or sheer lack of imagination:

> The child is pale and precocious
> She knows all the capitals of Europe
> She knows all there is to know about Wagons-Lits
> And First Class accommodation,
> But she has never been long enough in any nation
> Completely to unpack:
> Always her thoughts are centred
> On the nearest railway station . . .
>> 'Oh if only I could stay
>> Just for two weeks in one place'
>> Thinks the child of the doleful face.

> Moma has a cup of tea
> She is feeling better
> 'Cheer up girlie' she says
> 'I've a letter from your poppa
> It will take him some time to raise the bucks
> Shucks child
> Go and help nurse unpack
> We're here for two weeks at least
> Then we leave for Athens and the Near East . . .'[1]

Fortunately many children show remarkable resilience, and those in 'Advice to Young Children' would seem to have got by unscathed:

> 'Children who paddle where the ocean bed shelves steeply
> Must take great care they do not,
> Paddle too deeply.'

> Thus spake the awful ageing couple
> Whose heart the years had turned to rubble.

> But the little children, to save any bother,
> Let it in at one ear and out at the other.[2]

And there is also the little poem 'Mother':

1. *Poems*, pp. 88–9.
2. *Ibid.*, p. 174.

I have a happy nature
But Mother is always sad,
I enjoy every moment of my life,
Mother has been had.[1]

The most appealing of Stevie's children is the little girl in 'Si peu séduisante'. This is one of the poems that slide smoothly to and fro between French and English — an effective procedure peculiar to Stevie.

Il était une petite fille de dix ans,
Si peu séduisante,
Que entra dans le wagon-restaurant
Pour retrouver ses parents.
Elle portait son school uniform,
Si peu séduisante,
And a perfectly frightful little pair of shoes,
Mais ses yeux, malgré des lunettes hideuses,
Étaient si pleins de bonté et de franchise
Que tout autre aspect of this little schoolgirl,
Si peu séduisante.
Really only made one like her more.[2]

Stevie had a deep love of painting, and might have become an admirable critic of the visual arts. She is equally percipient whether she is writing about Turner, about the significance of George Grosz in the pre-war years, or about the strain of cruelty in Spanish religious painting. Something more should be said about her drawings which, as I wrote earlier, are often so very much more than mere doodles — they are often little works of art in their own right. Constantly we find in her work a sensitivity of line and rhythm and a deep feeling for design and composition, whether in the bolder linear drawings or in those of a fragile delicacy peculiarly her own. There is not much to be gained by comparing them with those of Lear, although he produced a number which could almost be mistaken for Stevie's. Lear's usually have a greater boldness of line and

1. *Poems*, p. 195.
2. *Ibid.*, p. 435.

structure, Stevie's a greater degree of delicacy, though Lear's are by no means lacking in this quality. There is no question of indebtedness — Stevie's, I surmise, would have existed just the same had Lear's been unknown to her. On the other hand her drawings show a strong affinity with those of James Thurber, but it is impossible to say whether there is any direct influence. Although it would be interesting to see what she would have done with colour, I don't think that the gain would have been considerable.

Many of the drawings are very funny indeed, sometimes in both senses of the word. An obvious example of the ludicrous is the drawing to 'This Englishwoman'. 'This Englishwoman is so refined/She has no bosom and no behind'[1] — which depicts an

elongated female protecting her emaciated form from the sun's rays with a parasol. Stevie herself assured me that the lady in the drawing above for 'The Cousin' was none other than her aunt.[2] Not a very flattering portrait, one feels! The drawing for 'Ceux qui luttent. . .' speaks for itself:

Ceux qui luttent ce sont ceux qui vivent.
And down here they luttent a very great deal indeed.
But if life be the desideratum, why grieve, ils vivent.[3]

1. *Poems*, p. 68.
2. *Ibid.*, p. 116.
3. *Ibid.*, p. 154.

To end on a note of pure fun (well, perhaps 'pure' is not the precise word). Here is an episode on the first page of Stevie's second novel *Over the Frontier*. Pompey, who is of course Stevie, is in an elegant picture gallery in London:

'And by-and-by if you go round the corner there is that flight of stairs which has Venus at the top of it, and once there was a man that had got funny in his head with drinking a lot of Schnapps, and by-and-by he got up those steps and was stroking this Venus in a very deep-going and affectionate manner, he certainly had a strong natural affection for Venus and what more like than that he should go to stroking this classical plasteret to show how he was feeling this very deep-going affection that was so right and natural and at the same time so simply free and outpouring? But by-and-by the man that stood there in uniform, he was a very formal character, very hardened in the emotional arteries, well, see if he must not go and give him a great push that sent him falling falling down that flight of stairs where at bottom he fell a victim to a horrible whore'.[1]

This is quintessential Stevie — the quality of the humour is unique. Her slant on the incident is funny enough as it is. But her manner, her flexible syntax and other irregularities constantly produce delicious little shocks of surprise in the reader.

1. *Over the Frontier*, 1938 and 1980, pp. 9–10.

14

Voces Intimae

The title, cribbed from Sibelius's only published String Quartet, could
be applied to almost everything Stevie wrote. But the intimate voices
I have in mind are the purely lyrical poems and passages of prose,
many of them having their roots in those parts of the countryside
which she knew intimately from her early years, the Lincolnshire
Wolds, the Estuary of the Humber, and the country around Hertford
so easily accessible from her home in Palmers Green. We know,
however, that she frequently visited friends in other parts of England,
and she several times mentions Norfolk, Suffolk and also
Northumberland, 'country of my delight'.

From a visit to her sister, who was teaching in a school in Redesdale
St. Mary, we have the following beautiful prose poem:

> There is such an air of innocence about this soft grass and the
> great mild parkland, and the ancient soft trees, and the great stone
> that lies upon the grass, and the feather fronds of the summer
> bracken that I look up at over my head, and the dark green leaves
> of the rhododendron trees, that the happiness floods into my heart,
> the usual great happiness . . .[1]

1. *The Holiday*, 1949 and 1979, pp. 61–2.

This passage is from *The Holiday*. But even when confined to her home in London, she was by no means cut off from natural beauty. Her friend Kay Dick has quoted her as saying that Grovelands Park, Southgate, where she spent much of her time, was 'the source of inspiration for a great many of my deep country poems about lakes and people getting bewitched and enchanted. It's very beautiful and quite empty. You can see right over to the Hertford hills'.[1]

But Hertfordshire was the county she knew most intimately, that is to say the country around Hertford and down to the northern outskirts of London, not the western Chiltern fringe of the county. She explored this terrain with Freddy during their extended and latterly very painful relationship, and doubtless before and after as well.

> To begin with there was for us again all of the lovely countryside of Hertfordshire for our walks together . . . Oh lovely Hertfordshire, so quiet and unassuming, so much of the real countryside, so little of beastly over-rated bungaloid Surrey-Sussex with all of its uproar of weekend traffic to and from Bloomsbury. Hertfordshire is my love and always has been, it is so unexciting, so quiet, its woods so thick and abominably drained, so pashy underneath, if you do not know the lie of the land you had better keep out.[2]

This is very tendentious, I feel, and grossly unfair to most of Sussex, and to the glorious Hurtwood region of south-west Surrey. But let it pass! I share her feeling about the Hertfordshire countryside.

Just outside Hertford there is the confluence of three tributary streams with the River Lea: the Rib, the Bean and the oddly named Mimram. The last was, in early editions of the poems, the home of 'The River God':[3] Stevie withdrew the superscription later. That this innocent stream ever had a 'wide original bed' would seem to be highly improbable! I suspect that the Bean, with its delightful riverside walk, was her favourite. She doubtless partook of the lavish and delicious watercress teas, which were then available at the village of Waterford. The Bean figures in 'Cock-a-Doo',[4] a poem of great metrical subtlety and richly evocative imagery, with a disturbing undertone which surfaces at the spine-chilling close. In an early poem 'Brickenden, Hertfordshire'[5] — a village south of Hertford — she

1. *Daily Telegraph Magazine*, 1 October 1971, p. 46.
2. *Over the Frontier*, 1938 and 1980, p. 33.
3. *Poems*, pp. 238–9.
4. *Ibid.*, p. 536.
5. *Ibid.*, pp. 114–5.

laments the 'tragedy of unwatered country'. Yet another Hertfordshire poem is 'The Ghost of Ware', an evocation of the spirit of place and a cameo of unruffled tranquility;

> This is an old house,
> The river flows below placidly,
> I am enchanted completely
> By this ancient city . . .[1]

Stevie was born in Hull; and although the family moved to London when she was four years old, she returned to visit the Humberside area from time to time. In *'The Holiday'* Celia stayed with an uncle, the Lion Aunt's brother and a country parson, who lived somewhere in the neighbourgood of the pleasant little market town of Louth, on the edge of the Wolds, sparsely populated unspoilt wooded chalk hills, with Tennyson's tiny hamlet Somersby buried in the midst of them. This countryside, too, with its early associations seems to have represented a kind of Garden of Eden for her. Looking out into the moonlit night, she exclaims: 'Oh dark Lincolnshire how beautiful you are.'[2]

The estuary of the Humber, too, was for her a symbol of pristine serenity, with 'the general and noble feeling that the world is newly come'. The poem 'The River Humber' has only a faint touch of disturbance:

> Quiet in the thought of its felicity,
> A graven monument of sufficiency
> Beautiful in every line the river sleeps complacently.
>
> And hardly the dawn distinguishes
> Where a miasma languishes
> Upon the waters' further reaches.[3]

Sometimes Stevie wandered the streets in the vicinity of her home after dark, as she tells in one of the most appealing of her earlier poems 'Suburb':

> Down there I know a lane
> Under the padding rain
> Where leaves are born again
> Every night

1. *Poems*, p. 299.
2. *The Holiday*, 1949 and 1979, p. 100.
3. *Poems*, p. 133.

And reach maturity
In a remote futurity
Before dawn's light.
I have never seen
Anything quite so green
So close so dark so bright
As the green leaves at night.
I will not show you yet
Lest you should forget,
But when the time is come for your dismembering
I'll show you that you may die remembering.[1]

So much she could achieve with the simplest words, often of one syllable.

I do not think it would be excessive to claim for her what Francis Thompson wrote of Coleridge: 'He takes words which have had the life drained out of them by the common cry of poets, puts them into relation, and they rise up like his dead mariners, wonderful with a supernatural animation'. Much of the effect of the lines quoted above depends on the sparing use of punctuation — this economy will have been noted in many passages cited in earlier chapters. Frequent commas could have killed the lines by impeding their flow and spontaneity.

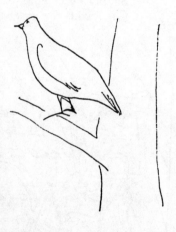

In 'The Old Sweet Dove of Wiveton' the bird's voice become a symbol of human love and human suffering. Here are the last two stanzas:

Now all is silent, it is silent again
In the sombre day and the beginning soft rain
It is a silence made more actual
By the moan from the high tree that is occasional,
Where in his nest above
Still sits the old dove,
Murmuring solitary
Crying for pain,

1. *Poems*, p. 82.

> Crying most melancholy
> Again and again.[1]

Another poem 'Nodding', in a different key, has perhaps an echo of de la Mare, especially in its last stanza.

> One laughs on a night like this
> In a room half firelight half dark
> With a great lump of a cat
> Moving on the hearth,
> And the twigs tapping quick,
> And the owl in an absolute fit
> One laughs supposing creation
> Pays for its long plodding
> Simply by coming to this —
> Cat, night, fire — and a girl nodding.[2]

Yet another intimate voice 'The Occasional Yarrow' concerns a brooklet which surfaces only once in seven years. I cannot forbear to quote the little poem complete:

> It was a mile of greenest grass
> Whereon a little stream did pass,
>   The Occasional Yarrow

1. *Poems*, pp. 365–6.
2. *Ibid.*, pp. 500–501.

Only in every seventh year
Did this pretty stream appear,
   The Occasional Yarrow

Wading and warbling in its beds
Of grass decked out with daisy heads,
   The Occasional Yarrow

There in my seventh year, and this sweet stream's,
I wandered happily (as happy gleams
   The Occasional Yarrow).

Though now to memory alone
I can call up thy lovely form,
   Occasional Yarrow

I still do bless thy Seventh days
Bless thy sweet name and all who praise
   The Occasional Yarrow.[1]

This idyll is a true Song of Innocence — was ever childhood more perfectly recaptured? One cannot help regretting that such beguiling lyrics do not form a larger proportion of her poetry.

1. *Poems*, p. 377.

15

A Smell of Poppies

Much has been written concerning Stevie's long love-affair with death, whom she regarded as a friend and as a god who would not fail her in the last resort, but who would come at the right time if summoned peremptorily enough. In his preface to *Me Again* Mr. MacGibbon writes: 'Her interest in death . . . was metaphysical and practical, not an ever-present preoccupation as might be inferred from her poetry'.[1] Hugh Whitemore has skilfully woven the theme into his play *Stevie*. Already, in one of her early poems 'The River Deben', rowing in the estuary of the Suffolk river, she muses:

Death sits in the boat with me
His face is shrouded but he smiles I see
The time is not yet, he will not come so readily . . .

Oh happy Deben, oh happy night, and night's companion Death,
What exultation what ecstacy is in thy breath
It is as salt as the salt silt that lies beneath. . . .[2]

1. *Me Again*, 1981, p. x.
2. *Poems*, pp. 48–9.

As we have seen, Stevie's existence was a prolonged struggle between the positive, life-giving forces of love and creativity on the one hand, and the negative downward pull of death on the other. And although this sorely-wounded spirit was sometimes tempted to give up the fight altogether, life had the edge over death. She was able to keep on partly by the fear of giving pain to those whom she loved, but perhaps even more by her Muse, which would not allow her to renege till she had fulfilled her mission.

In 'Why do I . . . ' Stevie wrote:

> Why do I think of Death as a friend?
> It is because he is a scatterer
> He scatters the human frame
> The nerviness and the great pain
> Throws it on the fresh fresh air . . .[1]

But over and above her longing for oblivion, to obtain release from the burden of consciousness, there is, I think, a basic psychological principle at work here, on which Miss Maud Bodkin, in her *Archetypal Patterns in Poetry*, has thrown much light. 'Medical psychologists', she wrote, 'have described the death-wish as an effort of the organism to restore quiescent equilibrium realised once (it is supposed) within the mother's womb; like the neurotic, the poet or his reader, dreaming on the river that breaks at last into the free ocean, sees in this image his own life and death . . . in accordance with a deep organic need for release from conflict and tension'. She quotes lines from Arnold's *Sohrab and Rustum* and comments 'We know from within what it is to be "a foiled circuitous wanderer", our own life-currents hemmed and split'.[2]

In what is perhaps the most beautiful of all her poems on this theme, 'Venus when Young Choosing Death', Stevie's passenger first encountered on the River Deben appears again; now he has become the ferryman:

> Then came one drawing a boat after him
> He set me in the boat . . .
>
> A little breeze drew now from the land
> Bringing a smell of poppies
> And on his head, was poppies

1. *Poems*, p. 508.
2. Maud Bodkin, *Archetypal Patterns in Poetry: Psychological Studies of Imagination*, Oxford University Press (London), (1934) 1963, pp. 66–7.

> And in his hand, poppies
> And on his lips when he kissed me
> A taste of poppies.
>
> Sleep or Death, Sleep or Death kissed me,
> Not for friendship.
>
> You do not kiss one for frendship?
> No, for welcome,
> To welcome one home.[1]

The note first sounded in 'The Frog Prince', an intimation of the second innocence beyond experience, becomes dominant in the final volume *Scorpion*. Although stress has not disappeared, there is a feeling of resigned tranquillity. Stevie is aware that release from the burden of consciousness cannot be far off. She has carried the child safely into and through adult life, and finally she reaps her reward. In 'The Donkey' she reveals it:

> Oh in its eyes was such a gleam
> As is usually associated with youth
> But it was not a youthful gleam really,
> But full of mature truth.
>
> And of the hilarity that goes with age,
> As if to tell us sardonically
> No hedged track lay before this donkey longer
> But the sweet prairies of anarchy . . .[2]

The feeling in these late poems is not, I think, far distant from that of the music of Mozart's last years: there is a peculiar sense of stillness. In Mozart's case, it has been described as 'deathly'. To me, the mood of his last Piano Concerto suggests a revenant revisiting the scenes of his past happiness. In Stevie's case, I think there is the feeling that she is passing into the antechamber of death.

> I should like my soul to be required of me, so as
> To waft over grass till it comes to the blue sea
> I am very fond of grass, I always have been, but there must
> Be no cow, person or house to be seen.
>
> Sea and *grass* must be quite empty . . .[3]

1. *Poems*, pp. 454–5.
2. *Ibid.*, p. 535.
3. *Ibid.*, p. 513, 'Scorpion'.

The note is intensified in 'Black March', a poem of delicate fragility which Hugh Whitemore has introduced most touchingly near the close of his play:

> But I have seen his eyes, they are
> As pretty and bright
> As raindrops on black twigs
> In March, and heard him say:
>
> I am a breath
> Of fresh air for you, a change
> By and by . . . [1]

This is one more small miracle. Does it come spurting up, ready-made, from the unconscious, as Mr. Larkin seemed to suggest? I am inclined to think, contrariwise, that the effect of spontaneous improvisation has been achieved by sustained and arduous labour.

The question arises: Did Stevie, or not, really crave extinction, or merely 'Oblivion', the title of another poem?[2] 'A cessation of consciousness' could mean no more than the shedding of a pattern of painful obsessions and memories:

> Though precious we are momentarily, donkey,
> I aspire to be broken up.[3]

Moving into nothingness can hardly be described as 'A breath of fresh air, a change'. For the first time she is looking past Death, her beloved, peering into the darkness beyond. There is deep regret in 'Grave by a Holm-Oak':

> Where have the dead gone?
> Where do they live now?
> Not in the grave, they say,
> Then where now?
>
> Tell me, tell me,
> Is it where I may go?
> Ask not, cries the holm-oak,
> Weep, says snow.[4]

1. *Poems*, p. 567.
2. *Ibid.*, p. 562.
3. *Ibid.*, p. 535.
4. *Ibid.*, p. 568.

Joy in living was by no means extinct in her: 'Oh grateful colours, bright looks!' is a small paean of delight in life, with a wistful note of hope at the end. It must be given complete:

The grass is green
The tulip is red
A ginger cat walks over
The pink almond petals on the flower bed.
Enough has been said to show
It is life we are talking about. Oh
Grateful colours, bright looks! Well, to go
On. Fabricated things too — front-doors and gates
Bricks, slates, paving-stones — are coloured
And as it has been raining and is sunny now
They shine. Only that puddle
Which, reflecting the height of the sky
Quite gives one a feeling of vertigo, shows
No colour, is a negative. Men!
Seize colours quick, heap them up while you can.
But perhaps it is a false tale that says
The landscape of the dead
Is colourless.[1]

This life-enhancing poem contains many of Stevie's most felicitous devices, and a delicious little colour-clash in lines three and four. It also affords an opportunity to mention one more of her affinities, the massive figure of John Cowper Powys, whose work, at long last, is achieving wide acceptance, and whom Stevie greatly revered. Although he produced little verse, his prose writings, fictional or otherwise, are permeated with poetical feeling. I am not, of course, suggesting that he had any influence on Stevie's literary style; but it is not impossible that the uniquely individual character of his imagination contributed in a small measure to her work. 'Fabricated

1. *Poems*, p. 546.

things too — front-doors and gates, Bricks, slates, paving-stones — are coloured, And as it has been raining now They shine'. This is essential Powys: in volume after volume he exhorts the reader to look for delight and solace in the most unlikely mundane places.

16

Sensibility and Sense

In this book biographical detail has been reduced to a minimum, but the poetry itself forms a kind of spiritual autobiography. I can think of no other writer in whom the life and work are more closely intertwined. At this point therefore I propose to scrutinize the novels a little more closely. Not only do all three contain passages of pure and at times splendid poetry — Stevie herself held that it was impossible to draw a firm line between what is poetry and what is prose — but they also illuminate the verse itself at many points. Accordingly a more detailed look at them seems essential if one is to present a rounded portrait of her as a poet.

The publisher to whom Stevie submitted a volume of poems in the mid-thirties told her to go back and write a novel first. Stevie wrote *Novel on Yellow Paper* in a few weeks and, on publication, it achieved instant success. Many readers were captivated by its originality, though some were irritated by the admittedly mannered style. Reviewing the book in *The Listener*, Edwin Muir remarked that it contained 'a well-developed picture of a disillusioned flapper's mind.' One would have thought that so fine a poet, with a wide-open door to symbolism, would have been attuned to the book's remarkable quality. On the other hand the undeservedly forgotten poet Robert Nichols was enchanted and was convinced that it was the work of Virginia Woolf; he actually wrote her an enthusiastic letter saying that it was easily her best novel.

Early in the book Stevie explains 'This is the talking voice that runs on, and the thoughts come . . . and the people come too, and come and go, to illustrate the thoughts, to point the moral, to adorn the tale'. And she warns the reader: 'This is a foot-off-the-ground novel and came by the left hand. And the thoughts come and go and sometimes they do not quite come and I do not pursue them . . . into a harsh captivity. And if you are a foot-on-the-ground person, this book will be for you a desert of weariness and exasperation'.[1] Happily its lasting popularity shows that there are more foot-off-the-ground people than one would have suspected.

On first picking up the book, the reader may be disconcerted by the inconsequent, often flippant style, and by the grasshopper leaps from one topic to another. Nor may he take kindly to being addressed as 'chaps'! But with perseverance the rewards are rich.

Stevie is essaying a new and spontaneous mode of speech; in spite of its oddities, and partly because of them, it tingles with life. In her second novel *Over the Frontier* the exuberance tones down; in its latter half, and even more in *The Holiday* written several years later, she reached a satisfying balance of manner and content. I am astonished that Philip Larkin found its style 'unremittingly artificial'. On the contrary I feel that it has a special quality of naturalness, and shows one personal way of revitalizing our glorious, but nowadays sometimes rather lazily used language.

Stevie was nothing if not English. In *Over the Frontier* she wrote: 'There can be no good art that is international. Art to be vigorous and *gesund* must use the material at hand. *Numen inest*¡.[2] And no one has better understood the English people. I think she especially valued what one might call our intuitive down-to earth realism and

---

1. *Novel on Yellow Paper*, 1936 and 1980, pp. 38 and 39.
2. *Over the Frontier*, 1938 and 1980, p. 66.

common sense, while at the same time balancing with ruthless objectivity our faults against our virtues. In *The Holiday* she wrote: 'The English are right not to make a plan, they know that the stream cannot rise higher than its source, they will not make an absolute plan to form man as a manufactury, they will not be so foolish and so wicked as to do this; they feel their way along'.[1] This of course, runs counter to the Utopianism that has been colouring, or discolouring, our thought since early twentieth-century prophets such as Shaw and Wells. Stevie was, I think, a truer psychologist, who perceived that we have to work with, and not against the grain of the nature of things: 'the stream cannot rise higher than its source'. She recognized that nations, like individuals, are what they are — one cannot change them radically by pressure. She seldom indulged in sermonizing.

Again she writes: 'We are vacillating, lazy and slow. We are not a sophistical people, and are saved from the dangers that run with sophism, and our education has not yet succeeded in taking away from us the weapons of our strength, insularity, pride, xenophobia and good humour.'[2] Stevie was well aware of the distinction between patriotism and nationalism. She probes the matter with subtlety in the later pages of *Over the Frontier*. The fine, moving poem 'Voices Against England in the Night', expresses perfectly the feelings of those who lived through the years of the War.

England, you had better go,
There is nothing else that you ought to do,
You lump of survival value, you are too slow.

England, you have been here too long,
And the songs you sing now are the songs you sung
On a braver day. Now they are wrong.

And as you sing the sliver slips from your lips,
And the governing garment sits ridiculously on your hips.
It is a pity you are still too cunning to make slips.

Dr. Goebbels, that is the point,
You are a few years too soon with your jaunt,
Time and the moment is not yet England's daunt.

1. *The Holiday*, 1949 and 1979, p. 9.
2. *Ibid.*, p. 90.

Yes, dreaming Germany, with your Urge and Night
You must go down before English and American might,
It is well, it is well, cries the peace kite.

Perhaps England our darling will recover her lost thought
We must think sensibly about our victory and not be distraught,
Perhaps America will have an idea, and perhaps not.

But they cried, Could not England, once the world's best,
Put off her governing garment and be better dressed
In a shroud, a shroud. Oh, history turn thy pages fast![1]

If England was 'once the world's best', what is the heritage that helped
to make her so? In *The Holiday* Caz says: 'The English . . . are
fanciful, as they are also sensible; there are two English animals, you
know; always against the lion of commonsense there stands the
Unicorn of fancy. This is not my own idea, he said; as a matter of
fact I found it the other day when I was reading that Indian chap,
the poet, critic, or something, I can't remember his name.'[2] J. B.
Priestley, probably quite independently, has enlarged on the same
idea contrasting the Lion of sense, guts and sturdy reliability with
the Unicorn of fantasy, originality and unpredictability. Both pervade
our literature, both are an essential part of the British genius, and
one fears, alas, that both are constantly at risk in this century.

In one poem Stevie displays considerable irritation with the Celts,[3]
but of course she would have been ready to admit the terrible wrongs

1. *Poems*, p. 216.
2. *The Holiday*, 1949 and 1979, p. 176.
3. *Poems*, p. 350, 'The Celts'.

which the Irish, Welsh and Scots have suffered at our hands through the centuries. Perhaps the Celtic strain in England is much stronger than is commonly realized, and the fantasy and romance which pervade our literature, (and without denying these qualities to the Saxons), are in large measure attributable to our Celtic heritage. Together with these are of course our vacillation, laziness and slowness, our foolish reliance on muddling through, which has on several occasions nearly been our undoing, as well as our capacity for sitting on the fence, while we pride ourselves on the English genius for compromise.

The more familiar one becomes with Stevie Smith's work as a whole, the more she grows in stature. Were Desmond MacCarthy alive now I feel he might have deleted the adjective from his verdict that she has a 'small nugget of genius'. Janet Watts, in her Introduction to *Over the Frontier*, speaks of that 'extraordinary unlimited consciousness that vitalizes all her writing.'[1] Stevie gets to the heart of things; she is also untiring in her pursuit of justice and truth.

I think that before concluding it may be well to emphasize again what is perhaps the keynote of her whole 'philosophy' or at least to indicate the root from which her insight stems. Everything she touches she illuminates. In Chapter 8 I quoted from *The Holiday* where she contrasted the intellectuality of early adulthood and middle age with the instinctuality of childhood and old age. Stevie went on to say 'It is the writer John Cowper Powys who has this fullest free feeling of the pleasures of *instinctuality*. . . . The feeling of full enjoyment will flood in again, we must get through these middle years.'[2] Here, once again, is the second innocence beyond experience, a kind of positive *second childhood*. And she returns to the same motif once again on a later page. 'Oh beastly mind that shifts so much, that is a tyrant . . . But close within there sits the soul in a crystal carapace that no claw can scratch that has no mark on it for all the mind's storms, that feeds upon the tears and the blood. And why should it not so feed? Is it not of God? sent out to be lost for a time? to return? So let it feed and grow fat, and return to God in admirable plight, yes, let it feed.'[3] It was the poet Paul Claudel who said, 'The soul is silent when the mind looks at it'.

However, her poetry is regarded in some quarters as that of a charmingly idiosyncratic, though sometimes deeply moving minor poet. I have attempted to show that she is a poet of considerable

1. *Over the Frontier*, Virago Press (London), 1980, p. 8.
2. *The Holiday*, 1949 and 1979, p. 124.
3. *Ibid.*, p. 200.

stature. And while in one sense she is a brilliant innovator, unique, in what she has to say and in her manner of saying it, in another she is a traditional poet, concerned with fundamental human experience and caring little for fashions, either literary or behavioural. But on no account must her psychological insight be allowed to obscure her gift for pure and original word music, or for the strangely evocative gleam of her imagination, together with her power to achieve high tragedy on occasion.

This short study has attempted to provide rather more than a bird's-eye survey of Stevie's poetry, though obviously it is much less than the definitive study which we hope to have sooner or later. I have tried to bring into relief important strands of her work, but have been obliged to leave out much. For example, I have had to omit most of the many poems based on mythology and Greek drama, or on classics from Catullus to Shakespeare and down to Henry James. But I hope that enough ground had been covered to enable readers to gain insight into this most unusual poet, a spirit both arresting and, allowing for the not-too-numerous 'warts', immensely appealing. In all her work there is manifest an exceptionally acute intelligence. I think, too, that we are now in a position to perceive something of the 'moral' and spiritual characteristics of her personality.

Perhaps one is impressed most strongly by a quality of *transparency* in her feeling and thinking, together with an intense passion for truth. She displays almost invariably a high degree of objectivity, a tendency to *balance*, to weigh up both sides of a question and to pursue truth by her own dialectical method of self-contradiction. In her capacity for getting inside the skin of her

characters she rarely misses the mark although, in a very small handful of poems, such as 'Valuable',[1] which strikes me as a little hard on the young women in question, and much more in 'But Murderous',[2] where I think she fails to grasp the woman's state of mind, I feel she is both harsh and widely astray. But such exceptions are rare. All in all, Stevie is revealed as a being of great humanity, warmly compassionate, and we know that she inspired deep affection in all who knew her intimately.

1. *Poems*, p. 447.
2. *Ibid.*, p. 337.

Index

Index